"Where there is darkness, let me sow light."

Prayer of St. Francis

LET ME SOW LIGHT

Living with a Depressed Spouse

Bernadette Stankard and Amy Viets

acta
PUBLICATIONS

LET ME SOW LIGHT
Living with a Depressed Spouse
by Bernadette Stankard and Amy Viets

Edited by Marcia Broucek and Gregory F. Augustine Pierce
Cover art and design by Tom A. Wright
Text design and typesetting by Patricia A. Lynch

Scripture quotations are from the New Revised Standard Version Bible, copyright © 1989 by the Division of Christian Education of the National Council of the Churches of Christ in the USA. Used by permission. All rights reserved.

All stories and quotations in this book are true. Names and circumstances have been changed to protect people's privacy.

Published by ACTA Publications, 5559 W. Howard Street, Skokie, IL 60077-2621, (800) 397-2282, www.actapublications.com

Library of Congress Catalog number: 2008931394

ISBN: 978-0-87946-378-6

Printed in the United States of America by Versa Press

Year 15 14 13 12 11 10 09 08
Printing 15 14 13 12 11 10 9 8 7 6 5 4 3 2 First

CONTENTS

—

To our husbands,
in celebration of their health
and in thanks for their courage.

INTRODUCTION
LIFE WITH DEPRESSION

—

When depression strikes one of the partners in a marriage, the spouse is also affected in ways that are often devastating. We can literally find ourselves with a different mate than the one we married. Alone and afloat on a sea of unfamiliar feelings, we question whether we have done something to cause this to happen. Could we have done something differently? If so, what? No one seems to understand or wants to talk about it. We feel alienated from our spouse, our friends and family, perhaps even our God.

Depression and its symptoms are a hot topic in the modern media. Advertisements abound for all the new "miracle" drugs now available. We've come a long way in the last couple of decades in bringing this illness out into the open. Depression is now commonly recognized as an illness that can be treated, not a weakness to be hidden. But the heartache felt by the spouse of a clinically depressed person tends to get lost as all efforts seem to be focused on helping the depressed spouse recover. The pain and the issues facing the non-depressed spouse are equally valid and deserving of help and attention. Depression too easily becomes a destructive partner in a marriage, creating feelings of isolation, hopelessness and confusion.

We know. Each of us has lived with a depressed spouse.

AMY'S STORY

Looking back, I can see signs that my husband Bruce had lived with depression, anxiety and other disorders for most of his life. It wasn't until he had quit a secure job, spent a year unemployed and ended up in the emergency room after disappearing for hours in an emotional blackout that he and I realized the full extent of his problems. What followed was a nightmarish succession of conflicting—and incorrect—diagnoses, poor psychiatric advice and failed experiments with various medications. Then came a twelve-year parade of mental health professionals, ongoing fights with insurance companies and financial near-ruin.

During those twelve long years, I felt that I lost many things. For an extended period, I lost my cherished relationship with my husband and best friend. Instead, I became a sort of parent to him, forced to take charge of nearly every detail of his life at a time when I was so wrapped up in our three small children that I had little left to give. Bruce was unable to work, and for most of those years I was needed at home to care for the children as well as my husband. Because of this reality, we lost our financial security. Perhaps most painful of all, I lost all trust in God. As the years dragged on and my prayer requests for Bruce's recovery appeared to be answered with a big "No," I eventually found myself incapable of prayer. I still believed that God was out there somewhere, but it seemed obvious to me that our family meant nothing to a God who could leave us in such a terrible place for such a very long time.

However, I also gained some very important things in those years. I found I could be pretty tough when things got difficult. I learned to trust friends with my pain and to accept help when I needed it. I discovered that I had a lot of staying power, that I truly had meant it when I promised to take my husband "for better or worse, in sickness and in health." In the end I gained a new, healthier relationship with my husband. And, though it took a long time, I learned to see the hand of God, guiding and nurturing us through those dark times into a new light.

BERNADETTE'S STORY

My husband Ed's depression was unusual. Because a strong work ethic had been instilled in him by his mother, along with an unhealthy concern for what people would think, he never missed work due to the illness. The rest of his life was another story.

Unbeknownst to either of us, Ed, from the time he was five following the death of his father, suffered from depression. The illness became his lifelong companion, lying just below the surface, waiting to take over. Early in our marriage, little things manifested themselves, things that in hindsight signaled something was amiss. Holidays and celebrations often triggered emotional scenes or withdrawals. As the years progressed, Ed became more and more unhappy. When he wasn't at work, he slept a great deal. When he was awake, everything took on unwarranted importance. For example, dust bunnies under the piano could be an obsession, and seemingly simple, everyday occurrences became major events. Ed tried everything to "pull himself together," but when he was unable to do so he plunged into an even greater depression. He tried all sorts of therapy, meditation and twelve-step programs, but nothing helped. When medication was prescribed, it proved a roller-coaster ride trying to find the proper combination. He took to trying combinations on his own, and I took to pacing the floor at night, ready to react should the combinations prove to be lethal.

During this time, I felt very much on my own. I had two young children who loved their father very much but didn't understand his reactions or why he slept so much. Friends didn't understand because they only saw the happy side of Ed and couldn't believe me when I told them he was depressed. After all, he didn't have any of the major manifestations of depression in public: Ed had never gone to a hospital with a breakdown or even missed a day of work. How could he be depressed?

I was alone and adrift without the support I needed. At times it seemed that even God had abandoned me. But God was silently at work: when I was able to separate myself from the illness, when I was able to give Ed the support he needed, when I was able to continue to be a good and nurturing mother to my children, and when I was able to see that I was not to blame for the terrible depression that had taken possession of my husband.

———

Both the authors of this book have lived with and, at times, thrived despite the depression of our respective spouses. We've found ourselves losing our patience and our tempers through the experience. We've said things we regretted. We've made mistakes. However, we have also learned many things about our spouses, our families, our God and ourselves. We have grown in understanding of people who struggle with this particular demon and come to realize that depression is an equal opportunity destroyer. We ourselves were a heartbeat away from being swallowed by the illness that once threatened to swallow our spouses.

We have come to realize that those of us living with a depressed spouse need the same care and support that is given to those whose needs are more readily recognizable. *Let Me Sow Light* addresses the pain you may be feeling as you watch your spouse struggle with depression and try to help him or her. We have also developed a website, www.depressedspouse.org, that we hope you will visit.

In the pages that follow, you will hear from men and women who have dealt with depression in their marriage. Though names and circumstances have been changed for the sake of privacy, these personal narratives come from real people who have first-hand experience with depression in their respective spouses.

It is our hope that their words will help you realize that you are not alone, that what you are experiencing is real and legitimate, and that it is possible for your marriage to survive in the face of this illness. We hope this book will help you find ways you can grow—and even thrive—through this time of challenge. And we especially pray it will help you recognize that God is ever there to carry you when the burden gets too heavy.

WHEN DEPRESSION
HITS A MARRIAGE

"For better or for worse, in sickness and in health, till death do us part." At the time of their wedding, couples make these promises and more in the sight of God and the entire community. In the newness and excitement of this celebratory time, even with the benefit of marriage preparation programs and/or premarital counseling, we rarely stop to think carefully and prayerfully about what these promises might really entail.

When we start out, we all have certain ideas of what we want from marriage. Our dream might be to work together with our spouse to build a home and a family. We may picture building careers together. We assume we will be equal partners in the sexual relationship, in parenthood, in finances, in decision-making, in faith.

As we grow in marriage, through a lot of give and take, spoken or understood division of labor, trial and error, and with God's guidance, we do our best to create the kind of union that is comfortable and satisfying for both partners.

In the backs of our minds, however, we know things won't always be rosy. We realize that "good times and bad times" will pepper the road ahead of us. But it is very unlikely that the illness of depression is something we expect or prepare for. Sarah's story reflects the impact depression can have on a partnership: "I grew up without a real father in my life. When my husband and I were married, even though I don't believe in 'the man wears the pants in the family' philosophy, I wanted a husband who would be a protective, father-like figure in some ways. That was how our marriage evolved, and we were both happy with it…until my husband's depression took over. Then I turned into the caregiver and protector. Everything was upside down."

At the beginning of the illness of depression, changes can be subtle, working their way insidiously into the relationship without either partner recognizing the signs until friction builds up to a crisis point.

Or the symptoms can be shocking in their boldness, stunning everyone. In either case, long before depression is recognized for what it is, both partners in a marriage are likely to have noticed many changes.

WARNING: DEPRESSION AHEAD

Changes in personality and in the marriage relationship due to depression are as varied as the people who experience them. The following is a list of early signs that depression may be affecting your marriage and might help you recognize changes occurring in your situation. Keep in mind that every relationship is unique, and that your individual awareness is necessary if you are to spot changes specific to your marriage.

• Changes in mood

You may notice a sharp increase in irritability in your spouse. Depression has been described as "anger turned inward," and this anger may boil over in the form of being hypercritical of others, especially those living in close proximity. You may find that you and your spouse are bickering more. Also, there can be changes in outlook. A formerly upbeat spouse may become withdrawn. As a result, you may find yourself feeling angry or irritated with your spouse, or you may discover you are suddenly "walking on eggshells" for fear of triggering an outburst.

• Changes in conversation

Conversation with your spouse may become one-sided. A depressed person may be silent and non-communicative. Conversely, he or she might start talking so much that no one else can slip in a word edgewise. You may feel embarrassed either by your spouse's apparent sullenness or by the way he or she monopolizes conversation in social situations.

• Changes in grooming habits

Depression often has an adverse effect on interest in and ability to keep up with regular grooming habits. Showering, hair styling, putting on makeup, shaving, choosing appropriate clothing—all these may begin to suffer. You may feel embarrassed when the two of you are out in public because of these changes.

• Changes in sleep patterns

It is very common for depression to create havoc with sleep patterns. Staying up later and later at night, and having more and more difficulty waking up in the morning, is a common occurrence among depressed people. "Most nights my wife goes to bed between 2:00 and 4:30 a.m.," says George. "We bought a second alarm clock that was advertised as being especially loud, but it didn't help. How can anyone wake up in the morning when they've only had two or three hours of sleep?" Disturbed sleep patterns, when they continue over time, seriously affect the rest of the family. When a depressed person ends up sleeping during the day, promised tasks may go undone. You may feel let down and put upon when you realize that you can't count on your spouse to function normally and have to pick up more and more of the slack.

• Changes in sex drive

It is also common for depression to create big changes in a couple's sex life. A comfortable sexual relationship may take on a different, unfamiliar tone. Frequency may either decrease or increase because of the depression. Sometimes depression causes people to feel so empty that they lose all interest in sex. On the other hand, sex may become a means of escape or a means of temporarily elevating mood, and your depressed spouse may initiate sex more frequently than before. Changes in frequency or expression of sex might cause questions to arise concerning your spouse's fidelity, when in truth it could be simply the depression that is causing the changes. You might even find yourself questioning your own sexual desirability or sex drive.

• Changes in decision-making ability

Depression often displays itself as severe confusion, even in seemingly small things. Decisions that were previously automatic, such as deciding what to put on a hamburger at a fast-food place, can cause consternation in a depressed person. Because decision-making becomes so exhausting, many depressed people end up choosing not to decide, insisting instead that others make decisions for them. A depressed person may also begin making poor decisions. Given a list of things to do for the day, for example, he or she might spend hours getting photos from last weekend printed and meanwhile ignore contacting the doctor to make sure a child's medication is called in to the pharmacy. You may feel more and more burdened by the responsibility of always having to decide things and by the need to compensate for poor decision-making on the part of your spouse.

• Changes in memory

Depression may affect short-term memory, and you may find yourself needing to repeat things to your spouse. For example, he or she may head to the grocery store with a mental list of two items to buy and then call twice to ask you what the items were. Frustration may start to build on your part as you notice more and more often that you're faced with a blank stare as you say, "But we talked about this yesterday."

• Changes in financial responsibility

If bill paying was previously the responsibility of the depressed spouse, that too may suffer. Large purchases that would have once been a joint decision may now become impulse buys on the part of your husband or wife. Depression can cause some people to turn into "shopaholics" as they seek a brief adrenaline rush from purchasing. "Every time my husband goes out, he comes home with 'the deal of the century' that he just had to buy," says Gina. "I have to remind him constantly that we need to operate under a budget, and we argue about returning those 'deals' that he brings home." As a result of your spouse's increasingly inappropriate spending, you may begin to feel that nagging about money or worrying about your budget is taking over your life.

• Changes in work habits

Depression may cause a person who used to derive a great deal of satisfaction from his or her job to lose interest in work or begin complaining about it. Your spouse may begin to be late for work more and more often, and excuses may become commonplace. You might find yourself worrying about whether your spouse will even be able to hang on to his or her job under these circumstances. On the other hand, a depressed person may start working longer and longer hours, trying to get away from the depression through work. In this case, you may be struggling to cover household or parenting duties by yourself and, consequently, feel overtaxed. Or a depressed person may decide, out of the blue, to pursue a career change. This sudden move, especially in light of other symptoms regarding work you may be noticing, may generate valid feelings of alarm or fear in you.

• Changes in parenting

When depressed, a formerly active, involved parent may begin to lose interest in his or her children or become increasingly impatient with them. Or the opposite may occur. Your depressed spouse may suddenly focus on the children to the exclusion of other responsibilities.

Or your spouse may try to step down from the parenting role and become merely a playmate to your children. As a result, you might find yourself apologizing to the children for their mother's or father's grouchiness or protecting them from your spouse's moods. If you find yourself handling most parenting tasks and decisions alone, you may be feeling worn out or resentful.

—

Have you noticed any of these changes in your spouse's behavior? If changes in your spouse have caused you enough concern to pick up this book, it's probably a sign that there might be problem. But keep in mind that, though depression may be an underlying factor in these changes, there could be other situations coming into play. An illness other than depression, such as an imbalance in medications, uncontrolled diabetes or any number of other conditions, could be a factor.

Taking an honest inventory of changes in the relationship, and how those changes are affecting the marriage, is a vital first step in facing the illness. Sometimes you may be the only one who can tell when things are not right. Though friends and family may be able to help by providing observations from a different perspective, ultimately you are the best judge—unless you happen to be in a state of denial. If that is the case, you may need family and friends to help you look at the situation more openly and honestly.

—

FOR REFLECTION

What changes am I noticing in my spouse?

What changes am I noticing in our relationship?

Could depression be the underlying factor in these changes?
What else could be contributing to these changes?

What differences am I aware of in myself when I am around my spouse? How do I feel about myself these days?

Symptoms of Depression

According to the National Institute of Mental Health, depression is considered to be present if five of the following symptoms are observed for at least two weeks:

Persistent sad, anxious or "empty" mood

Feelings of hopelessness, pessimism

Feelings of guilt, worthlessness, helplessness

Loss of interest or pleasure in hobbies and activities that were once enjoyed, including sex

Decreased energy, fatigue, being "slowed down"

Difficulty concentrating, remembering, making decisions

Trouble sleeping, early-morning awakening, or oversleeping

Appetite and/or weight changes

Thoughts of death or suicide, or suicide attempts

Restlessness, irritability

Persistent physical symptoms—such as headaches, digestive disorders and chronic pain—that do not respond to routine treatment

THE ELEPHANT IN THE ROOM

It's a fact of human nature that we tend to avoid change. And when change appears to be for the worse, we tend not only to avoid it but also to deny that it is even occurring. It can seem much easier to pretend everything is okay, compensating for any changes in our spouse, than to look at the situation for what it is, to name it and to deal with it. The "dealing with it" can appear huge, terrifying and foreign. So we have a tendency to tiptoe around that elephant in the room, hoping that if we pretend the depression is not there it will go away.

But if the elephant in the room truly is clinical depression, it won't just "go away." The longer we try to ignore it, the bigger and more destructive it will become, until our relationship with our spouse is so changed from what we originally experienced that it can be almost unrecognizable.

As painful and difficult as it is likely to be, at some point someone needs to take responsibility for identifying the problem and getting help. Often that someone ends up being you, the depressed person's spouse, who promised to stick by him or her "in good times and in bad."

A good place to start is with an open, honest, non-threatening conversation with your spouse about the changes you're noting and how they're affecting your relationship and your family. Many times, those in the throes of depression want someone to understand, at least in some small way, what they are experiencing. Though it may not be possible for you to truly understand clinical depression unless you have experienced it yourself, you can communicate your care and concern. Let your spouse know how sad you feel about his or her pain and how much you want to be a partner on the road to recovery. Assure him or her that you will be there each step of the way.

Suggest ruling out other possible causes or effects of what your spouse is experiencing, including physical illness, financial or work-related concerns, sexual difficulties, or other emotional problems. It is important not to discount the depth and power of the depression and to remember that it is often caused or exacerbated by genetic predisposition or chemical imbalance. Acknowledgement of this destructive force is important to your loved one's recovery and your own well-being and that of your marriage.

As the conversation continues, move toward the importance of seeking outside help in dealing with the depression. Offer to help find the outside support of medical professionals, therapists, family and friends. (And be ready to follow through on your promises.)

Though your goal for these initial conversations is getting your spouse to seek a diagnosis and explore treatment options, be aware that a depressed spouse is likely to find even talking about these goals overwhelming. While you may find the subject frightening, your spouse may find it almost impossible. Depression takes away a person's ability to face day-to-day reality and to make decisions— even decisions that might lead to getting better.

When a spouse is resistant to admitting the possibility of depression or seeking treatment, choosing your words carefully is vital. Becoming angry may be your honest reaction, and anger may come spilling out in a moment of frustration, but it will certainly be counterproductive. Instead, save that particular emotional reaction to share with a trusted friend. With your spouse, try to remain calm and talk about the depression as the illness that it is. Stay focused on the idea that seeking treatment is normal, that people do recover from depression, and that dealing with this life-threatening illness usually leads to a happier, healthier life. By taking your time, by removing your own negative feelings from the conversation, and by using gentle, non-threatening language, you may be able to help your spouse admit that he or she needs help.

This is not to say you should ignore your own feelings. It is especially important for you, the non-depressed spouse, to admit your own conflicting emotions arising from your spouse's depression. If, for example, you've been used to sharing (or even abdicating) responsibility for paying the monthly bills and now that chore has landed entirely in your lap, you might be feeling resentful. If a formerly thoughtful and loving spouse now criticizes your every word, you might feel hurt and angry. If your spouse has suddenly lost interest in and patience with children, you may be frightened as you begin to function much like a single parent. If your sex life has been affected, you could be resentful or lose your self-confidence.

When depression hits a marriage, both spouses suffer. As you watch the pain your spouse is suffering and try to deal with the impact of the illness on your relationship, admit your suffering as early as possible—to yourself, to a loved one, to a minister or medical professional—so that you too can take steps to deal with it. If you ignore or deny your own feelings, it's a sure bet they'll grow and multiply, crowding out any potential for a good relationship with your spouse. The elephant in the room will take over your marriage.

FOR REFLECTION

What might I need to say to my spouse in an open and honest conversation? What should I avoid saying?

How can I learn about treatment options? How can I encourage my spouse to explore them?

What can I do to pay attention to my own feelings during this process?

WHAT NEXT?

A good first step is getting your depressed spouse to have a thorough physical exam. If your spouse balks at such a move, discussing your concerns with a doctor, a mental health professional or a trusted minister may help you decide whether medical and/or psychological intervention would be appropriate. Considering all the options is important to the treatment of depression and the healing of your marriage.

"It's somehow easier for us to deal with an illness like cancer as an invader," says Dr. Stephen Samuelson, a psychiatrist in Kansas City, Missouri. "It's important that we try to look at depression in that way as well."

If you suspected your spouse had cancer, wouldn't you insist that he or she see a doctor and get help? Wouldn't you expect your spouse to do the same for you?

If your spouse is willing to talk to a doctor, a therapist, or a minister, treat this as a big step toward recovery. It is an unfortunate fact that depression is not always simple to diagnose. Unlike a disease such as cancer, which can be pinpointed through imaging, or diabetes, which can be diagnosed through blood and urine tests, there is no objective test that can tell if a person definitely suffers from clinical depression.

Because the diagnosis of this illness is so difficult, deciding whether to seek treatment and what kinds of treatment to consider becomes difficult as well. There are many decisions to be made that tend to require a lot of guesswork, trial and error—and time. A lot of questions arise, such as:

Is medication needed?

What medications do the doctors recommend?

How long will it take for the medication to take effect?

What will be the evidence that the medication is working or
not working?

If the first recommended medication doesn't work, how long
will it take to gradually and safely taper off it, and how long
will it take to find a new drug and get it to a therapeutic
level?

What types of therapy might be most helpful? Psychological?
Psychiatric? Marital? Family?

Where can we get a reliable referral for good therapists?

What if the first therapists we see isn't a good match?

How on earth are we going to pay for all this?

Entering treatment or therapy can be a daunting task. If
depression is diagnosed after medical and psychological evaluation,
you'll be entering a new phase that presents its own challenges. You
may find yourself suddenly inundated by appointments with various
doctors and therapists, along with an overload of information about
depression that can be confusing, even contradictory. It can all
become overwhelming pretty quickly, and the perverse nature of
the illness is that the depressed person is often unable to deal with
all the appointments, information and decisions that must be made.
That leaves you, the non-depressed spouse—who probably already
has a full life and a busy schedule—juggling a lot of very heavy extra
responsibility.

FOR REFLECTION

To whom specifically can I turn for referrals for medical doctors, therapists, courses of treatment?

How do I discover what assistance is available for dealing with my spouse's medical and treatment needs, including our financial needs?

Who is there to help support me in all this?

Depression and Treatment

Approximately 20 million Americans will experience an episode of major depression in their lifetime. This includes children, youths, adults and older adults. (Center for Practical Bioethics)

Approximately 80-90% of people who seek treatment for depression experience relief. (American Psychiatric Association)

Only 25-30% of those who suffer from depression seek treatment. (Center for Practical Bioethics)

Only 50% of depression patients continue taking medication as prescribed. (National Institute of Mental Health)

YOU'RE NOT ALONE

If your spouse is depressed, your closest friends and family members have probably already noticed that something is wrong, and they are likely to be your first line of support. You will need friends who can listen when you're worn out, people who can baby-sit while you go with your spouse to appointments, and family who can spend time with your spouse when you need to get away. But sometimes even the most loving friends or family members won't understand depression at first, and sharing the burden of a depressed spouse can have unexpected pitfalls as well.

COMMON REACTIONS

• "Pull yourself together"

Be prepared for those who subscribe to an outdated "pull-yourself-together" philosophy. "My in-laws were so loving and supportive to me when my wife was diagnosed," recalls Sam, "but they were impatient with their daughter. My father-in-law told me he thought my wife was just being selfish. My mother-in-law constantly told my wife that if she'd just pull herself together and get a new job she'd be fine. I kept telling myself that they didn't know any better, that they're from an older generation who don't really understand depression. But their comments were hurtful and didn't help."

If you run into this type of reaction, it may help to provide your friends and relatives (including children where appropriate) some up-to-date reading material on depression, its causes and its treatments. Education might change attitudes. Being truthful about the effect of insensitive comments can be helpful as well. As hard as it may be, you may find relief in saying, "When you say things like that about my husband, it doesn't help me or him. There's no quick or easy solution to this problem, and we need your patience and understanding."

• Disbelief

Another common reaction from others is disbelief. "Carol's suffering from depression? No way! She's always so upbeat!" It's a strange thing about depression: Many times the depressed person manages to appear happy, gregarious and "together" in public. Then, at home, the same person turns morose, critical and unable to think clearly. When this is the case, not only is it hard to convince people that there really is a serious problem but also you might end up feeling hurt and angry, wondering why you get to deal with the "sick Carol" while everyone else gets to see the "well Carol."

It may be small comfort, but try to keep in mind the likely reason for this behavior. In public, your spouse feels pressure to perform, to fit everyone's expectations. With you, your spouse may feel safer, knowing he or she has your unconditional love. With you, there is no need to put on pretenses. In public, an "act" is necessary. At home, there is freedom to let his or her true feelings show, even if it makes it more difficult on you and your children.

• The "experts"

Some people may try to minimize the magnitude of the problems caused by depression. Antidepressants are so much in the media these days that everyone seems to be an expert on their effectiveness. "Sometimes it seemed as if everyone with whom I shared my husband's illness knew someone who had beaten depression quickly and easily by taking the latest drug," Sarah says. "I got sick of hearing how easy it is to treat depression these days. It's not easy. At least it wasn't for us."

Though you can tell yourself that these comments are meant to be encouraging, they can hurt nonetheless. Here again, telling the truth can help relieve your feelings of frustration. Try this statement: "I appreciate that you're trying to be positive. But this is an incredibly difficult time for us, and I'm not feeling very positive right now." The burden can be lightened by not holding your feelings inside.

• Your personal deluge

And, of course, in the midst of everyone else's reactions you too are flooded with reactions: embarrassment (how do I explain this to people), fear (what will I do if my spouse doesn't get better), anger (why am I the one who gets stuck taking care of everything), grief (I miss the spouse I used to know), even feelings of being abandoned by God.

These feelings, and any others you may be experiencing, are valid. Try to give yourself permission to acknowledge any way you happen to be feeling. It is a good thing to realize that, even though you may not have a diagnosable, potentially life-threatening illness like your spouse, your feelings and fears are real and serious. Begin to seek ways to relieve your burden and care for yourself. Identify someone with whom you can share your troubles. Keep in mind, however, that though you've been living in close quarters with your spouse's depression, it may come as a shock to other people. Don't try to downplay your pain or the difficulties of slogging through every day life with a depressed spouse; tell it like it is. But allow your friends and family time to experience, accept and understand what is happening to their friend and loved one. Only when those who love you the most understand what you're truly going through will they be able to help when you need them.

FOR REFLECTION

What kinds of emotions am I experiencing as a result of my spouse's depression?

What reactions am I receiving from those who learn of my

spouse's illness? How do I feel about these reactions? How do I educate them about what is really happening?

What specifically can I do this week to keep from feeling burdened by negative emotions and reactions?

—

THE LIFELINE OF COMMUNITY

If you are feeling protective of your spouse and/or children, discouraged by other people's reactions, or confused by your own emotions, you might be tempted to withdraw from others and from the potential discomfort that "exposure" of your spouse's depression might bring. However, isolating yourself is not an option. It will only increase your disconnection from the very people and resources that might be able to help you or help your spouse. By allowing the people whom you define as your "community"—whether they are people from your church or work or family or neighborhood—to know about your situation, you are opening yourself up to the support only they can offer. You are making room for their gifts of caring and creating opportunities for others to participate in your struggle, rather than allowing yourself to feel more and more drained each day. The bottom line is that when you ask for and receive help you are no longer alone.

Do you know the story of St. Monica, the mother of St. Augustine? Before Augustine became a church scholar and saint, he went through phrases of severe depression and long periods of morbidity, seeking relief in excessive use of alcohol, sex and gambling. Monica took it upon herself, at a time in which medication and therapy for depression didn't exist, to storm the heavens for relief for her son. Year after year, she prayed and wept. Year after year, even when it seemed as if God weren't answering her, she kept her faith. She believed that God wanted a better life for her son, and she never gave up. And she kept reminding Augustine that there was a better life for him if he could overcome his depression.

In Augustine's later writing, *Confessions*, he talked of his mother's persistence, which became so legendary that when the early Spanish explorers in Southern California found a rock spring that dripped and dribbled ceaselessly they called it and the town they founded nearby "Santa Monica" in honor of this never-give-up mother. One of the reasons Monica was able to remain so steadfast was that the early Christian community around her was very active in its support of one another. Such a community can be a lifeline to you and your depressed spouse, as well.

"I remember when I was at my lowest, really feeling like there was nowhere to turn, I approached my pastor," says John. "I told him the whole story, about my wife and about how all the care of our infant fell to me, about how I was worried she would hurt the baby, about how I felt that I had lost my life companion. Everything spewed out. I remember thinking it felt good, but I didn't hold much hope that it would have any lasting effect. I was wrong. Not only did the pastor check in on me regularly, but three parishioners often called or stopped by, helping in whatever ways they could. For example, one of them would take the baby and send me out to do something for myself. Those people became my lifeline."

We live in a society that prizes strength, success and fortitude. This fact makes it all the harder to admit to others that things aren't perfect. If you're the kind of person who has been taught to be independent, to solve your own problems, to keep "family business" within the family—or if you are feeling that no one will understand or that you are not strong enough yet to share what is going on in your life—consider these words that Madeleine L'Engle wrote in *The Irrational Season* about her own depression:

> I knew nothing about psychiatrists, despite the fact that I was taking a psychology course, and it never occurred to me to go anywhere to ask for help. After all, my Establishment training had taught me to Be Brave, and Do It Myself. I had not yet come across Dean Inge's marvelous saying: "God promised to make you free. God never promised to make you independent."

If you ask for help from your faith community, you will benefit not only from any practical support people can give but also from their prayer support. Think of it as having a cadre of believers behind you, with Jesus leading the group: "Where two or more are gathered in my name, I am there among them" (Matthew 18:20). Even when you feel spent, with no energy to pray, you can garner strength and hope from the knowledge that others are sharing your concerns and are continuing to pray for you. Community serves to remind you that you are not in this alone, that along with God there are people who are interested in your welfare and the welfare of your spouse and children.

This both of us know from experience: No one can get through the illness of depression alone.

FOR REFLECTION

Whom do I consider my community: family? friends? church?

What does my community already know about my situation? How do I let them know more? Is there someone in particular with whom I could share more completely?

What do I need to ask others for? Am I prepared to accept their help if they offer it?

MAKING A PACT
(PRAYER/AFFIRMATION/COMMUNITY/TRUTH)
WITH GOD

Throughout your family's experience with depression, the question of God's presence (or lack thereof) may loom large. The effects of the illness might make it seem that God has abandoned you. As you begin to recognize the pain in your situation and attempt to grow through it, we suggest that you form a PACT with God. Making a formal promise to God around these four key points can be a significant help in coping with depression and nurturing hope that life will get better.

PRAYER

God is ever present; no matter what time of day or night, God is there. When no one seems to be around to help, or when you think no one could possibly understand, God is ready to enter into conversation with you. Through prayer you can stay connected to the One who loves you beyond all understanding.

Your prayer doesn't need to be formal, flowery or even coherent, only honest and heartfelt. When you find yourself frightened or angry, confused or unsure what to pray, you can throw that burden on God and trust that the Holy Spirit will do the praying for you, as promised in Romans 8:26: "The Spirit helps us in our weakness; for we do not know how to pray as we ought, but that very Spirit intercedes with sighs too deep for words." With God, you can feel safe and comfortable in letting everything out—anger, disappointment, fear, envy, repulsion, sadness. All these emotions and more have a place in your conversation with God. You can yell at God about your spouse's pain—and yours. You can express to God your fear of being alone and abandoned, of becoming a single parent with more responsibilities than you think you can bear. God listens and responds in day-to-day situations: through people who offer help; through unexpected gifts of comfort, relief and support. And even if you doubt that God can do anything about the situation you're in, make the effort to hand your burden over to God. It's too heavy for you to carry by yourself.

AFFIRMATION

As you struggle with this illness of depression that has invaded your life, as you live with fear, worry and feelings of isolation or abandonment, it is important to do all you can to remind yourself that you are worthy and loved. Make a list of all the good qualities about yourself. Recall the things that drew your spouse to you. Remember that when your spouse was well, he or she found much in you to love—enough to marry you. Listen to the ways in which your children, other family members and friends affirm you. As an old saying goes, God doesn't make junk. You are made in God's image and likeness and that makes you God's work of art. God created you a unique being and loves you for the person you are. Now, more than ever, you need to remember this love. Affirmation is especially important at this time in your life when you may be feeling no longer lovable even by the spouse you thought loved you. Use affirmations frequently to remind yourself that you are valuable and loved.

COMMUNITY

The light and love of community is always important, but community is particularly needed when depression has invaded your marriage. Not only will other people be able to help you through physical needs and challenges, but they can also be a source of emotional support when you so very sorely need it. In order to seek out others who will support you in this difficult time, you need to recognize who makes up your community. If you cannot list at least two people, it's time to return to a church, or get out and meet the neighbors, or reconnect with your family of origin or your in-laws, or join a support group for the spouses of depressed people. Reach out so that others may reach back. Accept help when it is offered.

TRUTH

For many years, the standard reaction to depression was secrecy, as if depression were a personal failing of which we should be ashamed. But holding on to this secret keeps those who love us from being able to help and brings only an ever-deepening pit of darkness. You owe it to yourself, your spouse and your family to bring your pain into the light of truth. Through honesty with your loved ones in words and actions, through honesty with God in heartfelt prayer, you can find the help you need to survive and grow through this time of trial. It is truth that will help you and those around you deal with the situation. It is truth that will help you do what is necessary for your own growth and the growth of your spouse and children. It is truth that will nurture the community that is so important to your growth. And it is truth that will build an honest relationship between you and God. No matter how painful it is, coming to grips with your true feelings and thoughts will help decrease your pain and get you beyond it. If you want to survive your spouse's depression, you need to be honest with yourself and others.

As you consider this idea of making a PACT with God, it's important to remember that a pact is between two parties. God's part of the pact is already made: "I will never leave you or forsake you" (Hebrews 13:5); "Remember, I am with you always, to the end of the age" (Matthew 28:20). Don't underestimate God's interest and concern. Your marriage promises were made before God, and God wants to help you through difficult times. Though it may not seem possible just now, try to remember that God wants you and your spouse to come through this dark time together. Make your pact with God even in the face of doubt, trusting that God's pact with you is rock solid.

FOR REFLECTION
Where do I stand with God in all this? Where do I want to stand?

How do I feel about making a PACT with God, even if I don't feel ready or sure? What would being prayerful, affirming, community-mindful and truthful do for me?

In my own words, what will my pact with God look like?

DEPRESSION'S EFFECTS
ON CHILDREN

Childhood should be a time for growth, a time for learning through play, a time of assurance of the love of significant adults, a time of fun. But when children share their homes with a depressed parent, a carefree and secure childhood can get lost.

"My dad would come home every night from work, and after dinner he would sit in front of the television and stare," relates John when he speaks of his childhood spent under the cloud of his depressed father. "Night after night it was the same. I could tell my mother was upset on some nights, resigned on others. Some nights she would take me out of the house, and we didn't come home until well after Dad was in bed. I always wondered on those nights why my dad never worried about us."

Children are quick to pick up on changes in the family situation. They respond happily when Mom or Dad are obviously feeling good. Picking up on depression is no different.

Children in the family often respond to the changes going on around them by "acting out." Sensing discord, they display their worries through negative behavior. Or they may be so frightened by the deterioration of their family life that they withdraw, trying to hide from what scares them. Some children will side with one parent or the other, trying to protect one parent from the anger and frustration of the other. Or children may adopt the non-depressed parent's frustration and anger as their own, taking sides against the depressed parent. To head off "acting out," worries, fears and guilt feelings in your children, it is very important to be open and honest with them about the nature of depression and the changes it has caused in their mother or father.

DISCUSSING DEPRESSION WITH YOUR CHILDREN

Any serious problem that is kept in the dark grows and festers out of all proportion for children. Depression is no exception. Things only get worse if a parent's depression isn't brought out into the open within the family. Children need to be told about their parent's depression, assured that it is not their fault and nurtured during this time.

If depression in a parent is not explained, children often blame themselves. They tend to lack the emotional maturity to separate themselves from events that occur close to them. If Mommy is grumpy and impatient, hiding in her bedroom much of the day, children may conclude that they've done something wrong. When Mommy's strange behavior continues day after day, and no one explains the causes of these changes in behavior, this self-blame can become frightening and overwhelming.

"It was my fault," recalls Michelle of her childhood with a depressed mother. "I was sure of it. I believed my mom was unhappy because I 'chased my dad away.' In reality, he had died, but I wasn't told that. My mom was depressed because she was widowed at forty-two. I didn't have anything to do with it, but for many years I was convinced that her unhappiness was my fault."

It's part of human nature that when we have a worry on our mind we need to get it out. We may journal about it, make a list of steps to overcome it, or talk it over with a friend. Stating a worry out loud can help make it smaller, more manageable. The same principle applies to children. When we say out loud, "Mommy has an illness that causes her to act this way," our children can recognize that the illness of depression is something that happens, not something they cause. This allows them to experience a sense of relief that can give them the strength to move toward healing. And we parents can stop wasting our energy on hiding and pretending and funnel it toward constructive actions.

Jesus says it best in the book of John: "The truth will make you free" (John 8:32). We need to be open with our children about their parent's illness and how it can affect everyone's life. But obviously a preschooler's ability to process and live with this information is vastly different from that of a teenager. And no two children, even within the same family, are exactly the same in emotional make-up or personality. How you approach the subject with your children depends greatly on their age and who they are.

• Infants and toddlers

Babies and toddlers, with few or barely-budding language skills, are unlikely to benefit from any level of conversation about depression in a parent. At this age, your children are completely dependent on you for their understanding of the world, which for now consists only of their family and their place in it. They need to be assured that, no matter how uncomfortable life may become as a result of depression, they are valued and loved unconditionally. The healthy parent is the communicator of God's love during this period, and that love needs to be full and given without any strings attached. It is also important to be mindful of the infant's and toddler's ability to sense disharmony and unhappiness. Loving touch and constant reassurance of their value to you are much more important than words.

Infants and toddlers require near-constant attention from parents. But functioning as a single parent due to a spouse's depression can drain your energy and ability to provide the loving, positive interaction that very young children need. It can't be stressed enough: It's absolutely vital that you find time to re-charge and re-energize. Whether it's a prayer and devotion time in the early morning before the children are awake, a Parent's Day Out program once a week, or a coffee date with a friend while a neighbor watches the kids, you must find time to care for yourself.

• Preschoolers and kindergarteners

Preschool and kindergarten-aged children are beginning to understand where they fit into the world beyond their families. They are likely to have witnessed some kind of illness, even if it was something as minor as a cold. It may be helpful to discuss depression with them in terms of "being sick." If the symptoms of depression have resulted in a change in relationship with their parent, reassuring them of both your love and your spouse's love is extremely important. Be intentional—both in words and actions—about reminding them that both parents love and care for them. When and if your depressed spouse has high-functioning periods, make sure to take advantage of these times by facilitating positive interactions with your children.

• Older elementary children and preteens

Older elementary children and preteens may be more capable of understanding the difference between an emotional illness and a physical illness. They recognize that their parent doesn't have a fever or stomach problems, and that this illness is lasting over a long period of time. In addition, they're likely to know children who take medication for disorders, such as Attention Deficit or Aspberger's Syndrome. They have more familiarity with what sickness can or cannot do. Your conversations with children at this age can be more specific than with younger children.

Children in this age group are also very likely to pick up on the tension, anger and frustration that you may feel from carrying the burden of family responsibilities alone. They may take sides with one parent or the other in an attempt to restore harmony. "My mom was always mad at my dad," says Grant, whose father suffered from serious depression for many years. "I didn't know why, really. I just knew he slept a lot and didn't go to work like other dads. I knew he was sick, but Mom never got mad at me when I was sick. It was kind of scary. I felt sorry for my dad and tried to make him feel better."

Katelyn, however, took her mother's side against her depressed father when tensions arose. "Mom worked so hard all the time. She had to get a job when she didn't want to. She had to do all the housework and cooking and laundry because my dad was always either asleep or sitting around moping. I didn't want to have friends over because my dad was always hanging around in his pajamas. It seemed like Mom was always tired and upset, and I didn't blame her. It made me mad too."

Children siding with one parent against the other is certainly not an ideal family situation. These kinds of feelings mean children are trying to behave as adults within the family system, something they're not emotionally prepared to do. How can you avoid this reaction? First, you can do your best to keep some of your emotions to yourself. As hard as it may be to contain your anger and frustration toward your spouse, you can keep such feelings from tainting your children's relationships with either parent.

In other words, be careful to create and observe healthy boundaries with your children. You can be honest about how you're feeling without blaming your spouse. It's healthy, for example, to say, "I'm feeling tired and grumpy today. Please forgive me when I'm short-tempered with you or your dad (mom)." This is a far cry from saying, "Your father (mother) is driving me absolutely crazy and is no help around here at all!"

Also, don't treat your children as confidantes or friends. You can talk openly with them about the fact of depression in their parent, but you need to save your "emotional dumping" for adult friends and family members.

As your younger children grow older and become more aware of the negative effects of depression on the family, it's vital that you continue to show your love through touch and with words. With children who feel they've outgrown hugs and kisses, find ways to touch them that they can accept. Patting a head, resting a hand on the shoulder, rubbing a back—any gentle touch will mean something to them, even if they pretend not to notice.

It's also important to continue putting your love into words. Add "I love you" to "Good-bye" as you drop them off for school. Say it at bedtime. Write it in a note to leave on their dressers or desks. They need to hear it—again and again and again.

• Teens

Having a depressed parent can be hardest on teenagers. Teens are coming into their own personhood and are developing more and more relationships outside of the family. However, they also continue to look to their parents for support, direction and boundaries. When one parent is depressed, these needs may be overlooked. You may find yourself turning to teens in the family for help in carrying out day-to-day responsibilities, asking them to run errands, take their depressed parent to a doctor's appointment or care for younger siblings. Although responsibility is good for teenagers, it can become a burden if too much of it is placed on young shoulders.

Remember that even though age, ability and time say that teenagers are ready for the responsibility, they are still growing up. Every teen still needs to be a kid once in a while. Sit down and discuss with your teenagers what things they feel they are able to handle. Don't presume, for example, that they will always be available to take care of the little ones. Check with them about their schedules, and make sure that your family schedule includes time for them to have fun with friends, over and above their school activities.

Above all, make sure you talk with your teens about depression. Don't assume they know what's going on. Set time aside to discuss the situation with them and do so thoroughly. Answer their questions. Ask about their concerns. Discuss what the options for treatment are. But remember, they don't need to be burdened with *all* the worries that depression can bring to the forefront. Allow them to laugh and dance and know that life indeed is good.

• At all ages

Keep in mind that discussions about a parent's depression may need to be repeated, especially if your spouse's depression lasts over a long period of time.

"Brad's breakdown took place when our oldest was very young," says Sarah. "When we felt she was old enough to understand sickness and doctor's visits, we carefully explained her father's depression to her, but her siblings were really too young to 'get it.' And then Brad's depression dragged on for, quite literally, years. We lived with the swamp of depression daily. But somehow we didn't manage to discuss the illness with our children as they grew. I guess we figured that since we'd covered it once, everyone knew what was going on. It wasn't until the two younger kids were in upper elementary school that we saw a backlash of emotions toward their depressed father, that we realized we'd neglected to educate them completely about what was going on. We weren't trying to hide anything. We just weren't as proactive as we should have been. I think we could have avoided a lot of anger and hurt if we'd been more careful about discussing the depression with the kids as they continued to grow."

FOR REFLECTION

To what extent have I discussed—or do I plan to discuss—my spouse's depression with my children? What would be most helpful for them to know at this time?

How will I approach them individually? How much will I tell each of them?

What are ways that I can reassure them of both my and my spouse's love for them?

HELPING YOUR CHILDREN

Bringing depression into the open can create opportunities to heal some of the damage inflicted by the illness. Openness can lead to healthier, more productive family dynamics. Openness can also allow you to broach the subject of genetic predisposition for depression, which may be vital information for the future health of your children. In addition to talking, however, there are four additional tools that are important in helping your children cope: listening, routines, touch and reassurance.

• The importance of listening

It's important to be very intentional about communicating with your children during this difficult time. And listening is a vital component of communication. Listening to children involves not only hearing their words but also helping them to express the whole range of what they are thinking and feeling. It is important to see things from their perspective, not just your own.

"My son was five at the time my wife went into her major

depression," says Nick, a father of two. "When I talked to Matt about Mommy not feeling well, he would always look up at me and say, 'I know. I can't see Mommy now.' I thought he didn't want to be around his mother because he was afraid of the depression. Then one day it dawned on me: My son understood what his mother was going through perhaps even more than I did. The cloud of depression was so strong that Matt couldn't see his mom as he knew her. The cloud had taken her away from him."

Truly listening to children can allow their concerns and fears to surface. Some children are automatically afraid they will "catch" depression. Others are preoccupied with what *they've* done to cause the depression. Still others simply want to know why their depressed parent doesn't want to have fun anymore. By listening carefully to their specific concerns, you will be more able to respond to their needs.

• The importance of routines

For children living with a depressed parent, routine is all-important. Whatever the routine is in your house, do what you can to keep it going. Maintain a sense of normalcy. Keep the bedtime rituals and the prayers before meals. By sticking with routines, you will help your children see that, no matter what is happening, life will go on. Sticking with routines tells children that everything will be all right in the end. Whether it is homework, chores, visits with friends or family dinners, routines serve to reinforce the fabric of family.

"My mom was a good parent during my dad's depression," Helen relates. "She always had us sit down for dinner whether or not our dad was up to joining us. She always tucked us in, saying our prayers and singing our songs. One of the things she would say, especially during difficult times when I would express worry about my dad, was that 'Nothing is going to happen to us that you and I and God can't handle together.' That little slogan has helped me so many times in life to realize that together with God we could handle anything that comes our way."

• The importance of touch

One important tool that is often overlooked when it comes to children living with a depressed parent is that of touch. When a couple is caught up in dealing with depression, touch can be the first victim. Whether it's the goodnight kiss in the bedroom or little pats and kisses throughout the day, touch can be forgotten just when it's needed the most. Children, especially, need the loving touch of significant adults during this time in their lives. A hug, a hand squeeze, a pat on the head all signal, "You are all right, and people love you for who you are."

"During my wife's depression, I remember reading that touch was important for children especially in difficult times," says Tom, whose wife suffered depression following the births of each of their four children. "The article went on to say even if you just ruffled their hair as they passed by, that was an important touch. Let me tell you, my children didn't have neatly combed hair for over seven years. I ruffled their hair any chance I got."

Various studies have shown that touch is of key importance to the development of strong, healthy children. Loving touch helps them develop confidence and increases their ability to love others. When children are deprived of touch during a difficult time in their lives, their emotional growth can be stunted, perhaps even opening the door for the development of significant depression in their own adulthood.

• The importance of reassurance

For children of a depressed parent, reassurance is paramount. Tell them often that they are loved, no matter what. Remind them that their mother or father loves them, even if he or she is not able to show it at the time. Reassure them of God's constant love and care that always was and always will be there for them. Remind them that Jesus wanted children to come to him. When the disciples tried to stop them, Jesus said, "Let the little children come to me and do not stop them for it is to such as these that the kingdom of heaven belongs" (Matthew 19:13).

We are cared for very deeply by Our Heavenly Parent, who loves all of us. Whether we are living with depression, watching it as little children, struggling as a spouse, or coping as a parent, God will be guiding us as we seek to grow as family.

FOR REFLECTION

How well am I listening to my children? What can I do to increase my ability to really hear them?

What specific household routines are important for us to maintain as a family?

How do my children like to be touched? What can I do to remind myself to touch them often?

How often do I tell my children how much they are loved—by me, by my spouse, by God? Do I need to increase my reassurances?

WATCHING FOR DEPRESSION IN YOUR CHILDREN

Depression tends to run in families. At an appropriate age, children of depressed parents need to be made aware of the possibility of depression in their own future. This is not a discussion meant to frighten but rather to inform them, so they can be attuned to the possibility of depression in their own lives and be able to seek effective treatment. At the same time, reassure your children that depression is a not an illness that can be "caught." The reasons why it occurs are many and varied, and they certainly can't get it from a bug or from forgetting to wash their hands.

When your spouse suffers from depression, however, it's especially important that you be aware of and alert for symptoms in your children. Don't be too ready to diagnose everything as depression, however. Since you are struggling with your own feelings surrounding your spouse's depression, you may find yourself overly sensitive to signs of depressed behavior in your children. But if you do note a change in a child that causes you concern, ask for the opinion of another adult who knows that child well—not your depressed spouse, whose judgment is likely to be skewed at this time. Consult another family member, a teacher or a friend; ask for help monitoring your child. If necessary, seek professional advice from a counselor.

FOR REFLECTION

Have I noticed significant changes in our children's emotions and behavior?

Is there anything in those changes that I should be concerned about or pay particular attention to?

Who might help me be on the alert for changes in my children?

PARENTING HELP

Good parenting is a challenge under the best of circumstances. We need our spouses to help us deal with the daily issues of discipline, motivation and encouragement as we try to raise our children to become caring, responsible adults. When depression strikes one spouse, parenting styles and skills can be thrown into serious peril.

For example, the depressed parent may lose the decision-making ability that is vital in everyday issues with children. Poor decisions or indecision then can lead to resentment and misbehavior. Feeling overwhelmed by even the simple routines of family life, a depressed parent may withdraw, becoming unavailable to the children both physically and emotionally. A depressed parent, struggling with dark moods, may easily become annoyed, hypercritical and impatient.

Positive parenting can be impossible under these conditions. If your depressed spouse is already withdrawing from family life, he or she might be likely to withdraw even further or become completely emotionally unavailable, perhaps not even recognizing what is happening to the rest of the family. On top of that, if depression is deemed a topic that can't be discussed openly, your spouse may feel a sense of shame, leading to guilt, despair and a downward spiral that makes a return to a normal, happy and healthy family life seem unattainable.

All the while, you as the non-depressed spouse may be burdened by worry and shouldering increased responsibility for financial decisions, details of treatment strategies and a host of other concerns. Left to take on parenting responsibilities alone, or at least what may seem to be alone, the task may seem an impossibility. If you are stretched nearly to the breaking point, your parenting skills may begin to suffer as well.

Operating in many respects as a single parent, you may feel

angry and resentful over losing support in parental decision-making and the nurturing of your children. Feeling overwhelmed, you may lose your patience easily. You might even begin to exhibit behaviors that mimic depression: being short with your children, making poor decisions or finding yourself too worn out to make decisions at all. At the end of the day, you might roll into bed feeling defeated and guilty that your children didn't get enough attention that day, or worried over an expression in your child's eyes when your depressed spouse exploded with anger. You may enter a downward spiral of your own, born of exhaustion, fear and hopelessness.

Parenting children when depression is a member of the family is no easy task. The emotions you feel when this illness cripples your spouse can be intensified when you see it affecting your children as well. You may rail against the unfairness, wondering what on earth your family has done to deserve such pain. But Jesus sees the pain from another perspective: "As Jesus walked along he saw a man blind from birth. His disciples asked him 'Rabbi, who sinned, this man or his parents that he was born blind?' Jesus answered, 'Neither this man nor his parents sinned; he was born blind so that God's works might be revealed in him'" (John 9:1-3). The important message for you in this story is that neither you nor your spouse have done anything to "deserve" this depression. But you can both be reassured that God is working through this challenge facing your family and your parenting.

One important aspect of parenting while dealing with depression is how you will replenish your own reserves, which can quickly become depleted just when you need them most. It's critical to look around and see where you can find support and renewal.

Depression in Children

- When a child's behavior changes suddenly, the following may be early signs of depression in children: pretending to be sick; not wanting to go to school; becoming very "clingy;" exhibiting negative behaviors, such as sulking, seeming grouchy, getting into trouble at school (National Institute of Mental Health)
- Scientists have found evidence of a genetic predisposition to major depression. There is an increased risk for developing depression when there is a family history of the illness. (National Institute of Mental Health)
- Studies show that for each successive generation, depression is likely to begin at earlier ages, and that over the course of a lifetime the risk of depression keeps increasing. (Center for Practical Bioethics and The Mental Health Association of the Heartland)
- The rate of depression in children is an astounding 23%. (*Harvard University Mental Health Newsletter*, February 2002)

• Friends and family support

For starters, seek support of other adults outside your nuclear family. When difficult parenting decisions arise and your spouse is unable to provide help, turn to a grandparent or a sibling or a trusted friend. Not only can they provide emotional support, but they might be able to help you with discipline issues or give you a clearer perspective. Think, too, of trusted adults who might be able to provide loving child care when you need time away from your children and your depressed spouse.

• Self-nurture

In addition, it's absolutely vital that you take care of yourself—not just if there is time, or if everything else gets done. You need to make time for yourself each day, even if it's only a few minutes in the bathroom with the door locked or time parked in the car on a side street after the children are dropped off at school. Nurturing yourself is an important part of being present for your children during this difficult time.

"I remember I kept telling myself that I couldn't possibly take time for myself," says Sally, a mother of six children. Her husband was depressed for fifteen of their twenty-two years of marriage. "It seemed as if someone always needed me or there were always things that needed doing. But one day I realized I was spending time in the evening in front of the television, comatose, looking at junk but not really watching it. I didn't want to end up depressed too, so I got the idea of exercising while I watched television in the evening. At least that way I wouldn't be comatose. I rigged up one of the kid's bikes as an indoor exercise bike and started to ride it during the television programs at night. Soon I was reading magazines instead, and then crocheting and then writing. My first short story got written that way. I realized that in the little time I spent exercising I was taking care of myself. That made a difference in how I handled my spouse and my children."

• God's care

Then there is the most important resource of all: the God who created you, who entrusted your children to you, who knows first-hand what it is to suffer over a child's pain. God is ever ready to provide the love and strength you need to survive this difficult time. You can seek help from your Heavenly Parent, who certainly understands the hardships involved in being a loving parent.

You can also place your children in God's hands, knowing that God loves them more than you can ever hope to, remembering that God wants the best for them and will love them through any difficult times. You can trust that God's love will triumph over everything that fills your head and heart with worry.

FOR REFLECTION

What changes have I noticed in my spouse's parenting skills? What changes have occurred in my own parenting skills?

Where and to whom can I look for parenting support?

How can I take care of myself during this ordeal?

What will help me remember, during this tough time, that God really does care?

DEPRESSION'S EFFECT
ON FINANCES

—

A particularly cruel aspect of depression is its ability to destroy a family's financial security. Though depression strikes each individual differently, depressed people are often unable to work or they have a reduced ability to work. This situation can put a family's very survival—the basics of home, food and health care—at risk.

Conversely, losing a job, for whatever cause, can trigger a period of depression. Whether the depression or the job loss comes first, the result can be monetary troubles that couldn't come at a worse time. Just when a family is struggling with a debilitating and frightening illness that leaves no reserve of emotional energy, a non-depressed spouse often must also deal with difficult financial decisions alone.

DEALING WITH JOB CHANGES

• Unemployment

The typical symptoms of depression can read like a manual entitled "How to Lose Your Job." Inability to sleep at night can lead to inability to get out of bed in the morning, which can lead to arriving later and later to work. Loss of decision-making ability can mean bad decisions or indecision at work. The mental confusion created by depression can cause poor performance. Irritability and emotional outbursts can cause tension in the workplace, and business relationships can begin to suffer. If these and other symptoms of depression drag on over time, either because the disease goes untreated or because effective treatment is elusive, the result eventually can be unemployment.

The loss of a job can itself lead to depression. When forced out of work unwillingly, people begin to question their abilities and intelligence. They worry that they're unemployable. They miss the camaraderie of the office and feel out of touch with the rest of the world. It's no surprise that in worrying about how to pay the bills the unemployed often experience situational depression that requires extensive intervention in order to be overcome.

This effect can be especially pronounced for men. Stereotypical expectations in our society are that men should be the primary providers, breadwinners and protectors of a family. Though recent data shows that 75% of women work outside the home, these societal pressures for men still linger. "Since he's been unemployed," says Gina, "my husband, Gary, often makes comments about his much greater earning potential compared to mine. He reminds me that even if he took a job at a much lower level than the one he left, he'd still be making more than I do."

• Underemployment

Being underemployed can be another difficult issue. People who, out of financial necessity, take a job that doesn't require or utilize their level of training, education or skill, may find themselves dealing with depression brought on by this very situation. Those already suffering from depression may be dragged down even further by the prospect of having to accept a job they feel is beneath them. "Gary refuses to consider any kind of temporary, part-time job, even though he's been unemployed for so long and we really need income—any income," says Gina. "When I suggest that getting out in public, being active and meeting people might help with his depression, he denies that a part-time job could possibly do him any good. He feels it would just be demeaning."

• Sudden career changes

Sometimes those suffering from depression can sense disaster coming, and they look for an escape. Sudden fixation on a career change can be a warning sign. "When Sandy suddenly quit the secure job she'd had for ten years to start her own business, something seemed wrong," says Dennis. "I was worried, but I wanted to be supportive. But when that business never got off the ground, things went from bad to worse. Sandy couldn't or wouldn't see that her career change was a disaster. Now that she was her own boss, she could set her own hours and work when she pleased—which was less and less every day. Before long, she was sleeping practically around the clock. Finally, it hit me that the problem wasn't the career change. It was depression."

• Embarrassment and Guilt

In our culture we tend to derive a certain amount of pleasure and status based on "What I do" or "What my spouse does." If you're going to deal at all effectively with your situation, you will need to take an honest look at how you feel about your spouse's job and income loss. You might feel embarrassed or ashamed by a loss of buying power and status. You might feel frightened by an uncertain and unstable future. Or you might possibly feel relieved when a high-pressure job has lost its grip on your lives, but harbor feelings of guilt over such relief.

FOR REFLECTION

In what ways is depression affecting my spouse's work?

How is his or her work (or lack thereof) contributing to the depression?

How have I felt about my spouse's job? Did I feel I gained any status or prestige due to that job? How much does it matter to me what my spouse does—or doesn't do—for a living?

UNTANGLING THE FINANCIAL MESS

In most marriages, mortgages, car payments and insurance policies—
all the financial trappings of modern life—are a joint venture, based
on a certain expected income. As unpleasant as it may be to have to
look at life in such crass terms, money and finance play a big role. If
you're faced with a significant loss of income, you may also be facing
a big change in lifestyle—perhaps a smaller house, an older car, or
fewer or no vacations.

It's natural to feel concern when your family income is drastically
reduced. Depression not only can prevent your spouse from working
but also it can keep him or her from taking part in financial decision
making and bill paying. Suddenly, the person you have come to
depend on for friendship, support and help with the big decisions of
life is often unavailable for an undetermined period of time. He or she
is probably not even capable of supporting you through your fears and
worries about finances. You're carrying all the burden of finances on
your own. This creates unexpected pressure at a time when you may
feel your ability to cope is already stretched to the breaking point.

While it's frightening to see your spouse's depression worsen as
loss of employment and income becomes an issue, you might also
feel betrayed, abandoned or let down. After all, a big part of most
marriages is financial interdependence.

Even if your husband or wife did not work outside the home before
the depression took hold, there can still be financial consequences.
A depressed parent may well be incapable of caring effectively and
safely for children. In this case, costs of child care create tremendous
strain on income.

Of course, coloring this entire situation is the overwhelming fact
of the depression itself: You feel sad and worried for your spouse; you
want your spouse to feel good again, not only because feeling good

might mean a return to work either in or outside of the home but also because you want to see your loved one whole again. It may all seem like one big, complicated mess.

One way to start untangling the mess is to take a careful inventory of your feelings regarding income/job loss. It's important to recognize that when the scales tip in a different direction financially, the balance of power tips as well. Like it or not, a certain amount of power almost always accompanies earning potential. A spouse who has enjoyed contributing significantly to family income is likely to feel a loss of clout if that income disappears. A spouse who is suddenly responsible for all financial aspects of a marriage may have difficulty accepting that role and the power that comes with it. As relationships shift subtly, you need to be alert to your changing emotions. It can be extremely helpful to take an honest look at your feelings surrounding these issues.

FOR REFLECTION

What have we come to expect concerning income in our marriage? How does that need to change, at least for a while, due to my spouse's depression?

How are income and enjoyment of life related in my mind? What standard of living is really necessary for our happiness?

What role have I played in the past in our financial arrangements? To what extent do I equate income and financial decision-making with control or power inside my marriage? How is my role changing? How do I feel about these changes?

How capable do I believe I am when it comes to dealing with our finances and our reduced income? What concerns do I have about handling these issues alone?

ASKING FOR—AND ACCEPTING—HELP

Money matters tend to be considered a private subject. It's not an easy thing, in our consumption-crazed culture, to admit to financial troubles. You might even feel embarrassed or ashamed that depression and job loss have forced you to move to a smaller house, to stop eating out with friends or to trade in your car for an older model. You may feel as if you're saving face by not sharing your financial details with others, but the cost may be isolation and loneliness

As hard as it may be, it's important to speak the truth about what's going on and why. It's important to find someone with whom you can be open and honest about your financial struggles. Whether that someone is a parent, a relative, a friend or a professional (such as a not-for-profit credit counseling agency), having people with whom you can discuss options can be a big relief. Because you're burdened by all the other responsibilities you've been handed, you can't always see the choices available to you. If a trusted friend or family member is able to help with bill-paying or other financial details, this help can lift the burden and, even more, give you back some time and energy to handle the roller-coaster emotions of life with a depressed spouse.

One option to consider—and it's one that can be very difficult to accept—is public assistance. We have a tendency to think of Food Stamps, Medicaid and other forms of social welfare as helps for some "other" segment of society. But these programs are intended to be temporary relief for *all* who have been hit by unexpected misfortune. A depressed and suddenly unemployed spouse certainly fits this description. If it comes down to a question of whether your children will get the health care they need or whether your family will eat at the end of the month, it may be time to accept this temporary help. Keep in mind that key word is *temporary*. While you may need help at this time in your life, a time may come later when you can be the one providing help for others living through difficult times.

Each state offers and administers public assistance independently, though there are standards that each must adhere to for federally-funded programs. Wading through the different programs and their requirements can be difficult, but with perseverance and the help of a professional social worker you may find valuable assistance.

Some assistance programs are available in every state, while others are state-specific. Even those that are federally funded are administered by individual states, which means details of eligibility, application processes and amount of assistance available vary depending upon the state in which you live. The best way to discover what types of assistance you may qualify for is to check with your state social service agency, either through the phone book or on the internet. Your public library may be able to direct you to the appropriate agencies to contact as well. The following list of public assistance resources offers information about specific programs that may be available to you.

United Way 2-1-1: This simple telephone number helps connect callers to health and human services benefits available in their community. According to www.211.org, the United Way 2-1-1 number was serving over 65% of the U.S. population by October 2006.

The Cost of Depression

The estimated cost to society from depression is 44 billion dollars per year, second only to cancer and approximately the same as the cost of heart disease or of AIDS. (Center for Practical Bioethics and The Mental Health Association of the Heartland)

Food Stamps: Food Stamps is a program of the United States Department of Agriculture and is available in all states. Check with your state social service agency for details. For general information, visit www.fns.usda.gov/fsp/.

WIC: The full name for this program is The Special Supplemental Nutrition Program for Women, Infants and Children. A program of the United States Department of Agriculture, it provides nutritious food, health-care referrals and information about nutrition to low-income women, infants and children up to age five. Check with your state social service agency for details. For general information, visit www.fns.usda.gov/wic/.

Medicaid: Medicaid medical benefits are available in every state. Eligibility and benefit amounts vary widely. The website www.cms.hhs.gov/MedicaidGenInfo/ provides a general overview of Medicaid programs. Links on the site guide the user toward specific information for each state.

State health programs: Most states offer low-cost medical insurance programs for children whose families do not qualify for Medicaid. Check with your state social service agency for details. Your neighborhood school nurse may be able to provide you with information as well.

HUD Assistance: If you are behind on your mortgage payments and your home was purchased with a Federal Housing Assistance loan, the department of Housing and Urban Development can help you avoid foreclosure. For more information, visit www.hud.gov/foreclosure/index.cfm.

Social Security Disability: It is possible, though not easy, for people disabled due to depression to receive Social Security Disability benefits. Be aware that the application process is long and complicated, and that qualifying for benefits often requires multiple application processes. Consider enlisting the help of your state's legal aid services for low-income families. For more information on Social Security Disability, visit www.ssa.gov/disability/.

Free and reduced school lunch programs: The National School Lunch Program is provided by the United States Department of Agriculture. Qualification is based on income. For more information, contact your local school or visit www.fns/usda/gov/cnd/lunch/.

TANF: Temporary Assistance for Needy Families, a program of the United States Department of Health and Human Services, provides cash assistance for needy families. Eligibility requirements and benefits vary widely from state to state. Check with your state social service agency for details. For a general overview of the program, visit www.acf.hhs.gov/programs/ofa/.

Child care assistance: Many states offer assistance with child care costs for low-income families. Eligibility requirements and benefits vary widely from state to state. Check with your state social service agency for details.

LIEAP: The Low Income Energy Assistance Program is a program of the United States Department of Health and Human Services. It helps eligible homeowners pay their home heating or cooling bills. For specific details, check with your state social service agency or your local utility company. For a general overview of the program, visit www.acf.hhs.gov/programs/liheap/.

FMLA: The Family and Medical Leave Act of 1993 requires that
covered employers of eligible employees provide up to a total of 12
workweeks of unpaid leave during any 12-month period for one or
more of the following reasons: the birth and care of the newborn
child of the employee; placement with the employee of a son or
daughter for adoption or foster care; to care for an immediate family
member (spouse, child, or parent) with a serious health condition; or
to take medical leave when the employee is unable to work because
of a serious health condition. For specific details about "covered
employers" and "eligible employees," visit www.dol.gov/esa/whd/
fmla.

When serious financial concerns are added to the frightening realities
of life with a depressed spouse, the burden can become overwhelming.
If you feel driven to despair by worries over the basics of food, clothing
and shelter, compounded by worries for your spouse, it is vital to
remember that help is available—and to ask for it. Turn to trusted
friends and loved ones for emotional and practical support. Seek
temporary financial assistance. Most importantly, remind yourself
that you can trust your loving God to care for your needs, even when
you are in a place so painful you may forget to ask. Re-read Jesus'
promise in his classic "Sermon on the Mount" with new eyes:

> Therefore I tell you, do not worry about your life, what
> you will eat or what you will drink, or about your body,
> what you will wear. Is not life more than food, and the
> body more than clothing? Look at the birds of the air; they
> neither sow nor reap nor gather into barns, and yet your
> heavenly Father feeds them. Are you not of more value than

they? And can any of you by worrying add a single hour to your span of life? And why do you worry about clothing? Consider the lilies of the field, how they grow; they neither toil nor spin, yet I tell you, even Solomon in all his glory was not clothed like one of these. But if God so clothes the grass of the field, which is alive today and tomorrow is thrown into the oven, will he not much more clothe you—you of little faith? Therefore do not worry, saying "What will we eat?" or "What will we drink?" or "What will we wear?"... Your heavenly Father knows that you need all these things. (Matthew 6:25-32)

FOR REFLECTION

How do I feel about discussing our financial situation—and my feelings about it—with others? To whom might I turn for help?

What public assistance resources do I need to do to check out? When will I do so?

Do I believe that God is truly present with me in this crisis? If so, how can I let go of my own concerns and let God take over?

DEPRESSION'S EFFECT
IN THE BEDROOM

—

Sex. This little three-letter word raises a huge variety of emotions in everyone's life. There are those who talk openly and candidly about it. Others see it as a taboo subject. When things are going well in a marriage, sex becomes a fun expression of love and affection. Book upon book has been written about how sex is good for a marriage and how to make it better. Unfortunately, equal time is not given to how sex can be a real problem for couples living with depression.

Depression's adverse effects on life don't stop at the bedroom door. In the bedroom particularly, you may find yourself drifting further apart at the very time when you and your spouse need each other the most. You can lose not only the intimacy of sex, which provides a close, emotional experience that is reassuring and comforting, but also the physical benefit of the increased endorphins released by sex that elevate your mood.

Worse, sexual problems can raise doubts in you, or your spouse, about the other's faithfulness.

If you are experiencing changes in your sexual relationship with your depressed spouse, you may recognize some or all of the problems discussed in this chapter. Perhaps you will find comfort in knowing that you are not alone and will discover some ways to deal with the sexual issues that may be arising in your marriage. Keep in mind, though, that not all couples experience these types of problems. If sexual issues are not a factor in your spouse's depression, say a prayer of thanks and don't spend time and energy worrying that these things might happen to you.

WHERE'S THE ROMANCE?

Depressed people often feel withdrawn, and it is difficult for them to get the energy together to perform even simple tasks. Consequently, relating physically may become overwhelming. The little things that contribute to a good physical relationship may go by the wayside. The little kisses, the hugs, the intimate conversation—all can be casualties of the illness.

A large number of people who are depressed lose interest in sex entirely. In fact, many antidepressants can cause a loss of libido that suppresses interest in sex. Many times depressed people no longer have any desire to express their love to their partner, or if they do, those expressions can end up feeding the depression rather than helping.

"I felt like I had failed again," says Tom, who suffered through depression for over ten years. "My wife deserved a partner who appreciated her and wanted to make mad, passionate love to her, but instead I was absolutely not interested in making that happen. It seemed the furthest thing from my mind, and when I did allow myself to think about it, I was overwhelmed with feelings of inadequacy and failure. Either way I looked at the subject of sex, I couldn't win."

This feeling of failure and disinterest complicates the lives of spouses suffering from depression. Unable to engage in the act of intercourse because of the inability to achieve or maintain an erection or reach orgasm can often cause frustration and increase loneliness. It is difficult enough to feel lovable when your loved one has lost the ability to carry on conversations with you, doesn't smile at your jokes any more and doesn't seem to appreciate any of the good moments in life. To lose physical intimacy on top of that may feel like one blow too many.

It is important to remember that this loss of interest in sex has nothing to do with you. It is also helpful to be aware that if the person you thought you knew and loved begins to act strangely in the bedroom and seems so very unhappy, crazy thinking can be your initial response. The disinterest and self-centeredness coming from your ill spouse might encourage your suspicion of an affair, or you might begin to believe that your spouse no longer loves you.

Mike adored his wife Joan and had great times with her, both inside and outside of the bedroom. Sex for them was a great release, a deep expression of their care for one another and a source of intimacy. When Joan's occasional blue mood deepened into a full-fledged depression, Mike could not understand why she didn't have any interest in sex. He felt that it was one way in which she could know that she was still lovable, that he could reassure her that things would be all right, and that he was there to support and care for her. However, as her depression worsened, Joan repeatedly refused sex, and Mike's worries deepened.

"I thought she no longer loved me," Mike says. "I was sure there was someone else. We used to have such great times in the bedroom, and we always felt closer to one another afterward. Now she never initiates sex, and when I do there is always a reason why she doesn't want to. I'm ashamed to say that arguments have ensued because of it."

In most instances, the ill spouse doesn't love his or her partner any less. Remind yourself as many times as necessary that these symptoms are a consequence of the illness.

FOR REFLECTION

How do I view sex? How was it viewed by my family of origin? How is it viewed by my present family?

What changes, if any, have taken place in our sexual experience since the start of depression? How do I feel about these changes?

How I can I remember that any changes could be due to the illness of my spouse rather than any failing on either of our parts?

CHANGES IN SEXUAL EXPRESSION

Sometimes sex can take a totally different turn during depression. Sexual expression can become a way to avoid the demands of relationship, shed the repression of the disease and find a way to get relief, if only for a few moments. This might express itself in experimentation with pornography, in different sexual behaviors such as bondage, or in promiscuity. Remember: These behaviors reflect the illness, not any failing on your part.

• Pornography

Some people experiencing depression wish to avoid the demand for a relationship and consequently begin to explore and gain satisfaction from the area of pornography. With pornography, the participant does not have to meet the needs of a real relationship—it is purely a way to satisfy physical needs without the entanglements that a love relationship brings. However, if this is an avenue your spouse begins to explore, it is easy for you to experience this as rejection.

"I felt violated and very hurt when I discovered my husband was looking regularly and satisfying himself through pornography," recalls Janelle, whose husband continues to suffer with depression. "He would go and surf the web, finding all sorts of pictures that turned him on, masturbating right there at the computer. I felt as if he was having an affair. Part of me could rationally set it aside and see that this was merely a release for him, but the other part of me felt wounded that he seemed to prefer these other 'women' to me."

• Bondage

Some individuals deal with sexual desire during depression through the use of bondage, in which pleasure and orgasm are achieved only if one or the other partner is restrained in some way.

"When I would tie up my wife and make her helpless, it became such a turn on," says Jon, "that I felt an actual physical and emotional release. For that time, I felt good. I wasn't feeling the depression. I felt like someone had taken my bonds and had cut them."

Bondage in sex can provide a needed release for depressed people from the personal mental bondage they are experiencing because of the depression, but it can also be hard for a spouse to accept. When bondage expresses itself during depression, it can cause arguments and frustration. If your depressed spouse is pushing for this practice and you don't wish to engage in it, frustration can build for both of you.

"I just couldn't agree to it," said Mark, whose wife wanted bondage as part of their sexual experience. "She acted so strange at so many times and in so many aspects of her life that I was frankly afraid of what might happen if I was restrained and she went crazy. I wanted to help her, but I felt I had to draw the line at this point."

If you find yourself in this situation, don't feel guilty if you don't feel comfortable with bondage. Although your depressed spouse might find release in such an act, it is important that you be honest in expressing your own needs and concerns. If you do decide to engage in bondage, you and your spouse need to set ground rules about what will and won't take place. It is also of paramount importance to agree to a "safe word" that, when spoken, puts an immediate end to the bondage. In this way, both of you can feel safe. Ongoing discussion is important so both of you can find ways to meet the other's needs without sacrificing your own feelings or worries.

• Promiscuity

Still another expression of sexual need during depression is sexual promiscuity, which might manifest itself in one-night stands or sexual addiction. When this occurs, sex suddenly becomes all-important for the depressed person. This kind of sexual addiction might afford a pleasurable distraction and relief from the overwhelmingly negative feelings depression brings.

"I really didn't want to hurt my husband," Denise recalls, "but I wanted relief. I wanted someone who I didn't have an obligation to. I wanted the release that sex gave without the complication of a relationship. I couldn't handle that."

While sexual promiscuity may offer the depressed individual an opportunity to forget for a brief time, it is obviously destructive to the marriage. In addition, it opens the couple to the possibility of sexually transmitted diseases.

"I was so hurt," says Jane. "I had been trying hard to be understanding and supportive—and then this. He didn't want to have sex with me. He wanted a hooker. I could no longer be understanding of the depression. I thought he was just doing all this to hurt me. And God only knows what he brought home. Not only do I have this depression to ride through, but he might have brought home AIDS as well. I wondered time and again how he just didn't care. In my head I knew it was the illness, but my heart was saying other things."

Depression and Sexual Dysfunction

While labels on antidepressants state that approximately 15% of patients experience sexual side effects, 70% of patients, when asked directly, actually report having sexual side effects. (Brown University Psychopharmacology Update)

If your depressed spouse is seeking promiscuity as a relief, you may be thinking that he or she doesn't care about your relationship, about your children, about your life together. The marriage relationship, already hurt by so many challenges, is now faced with the destructive force of infidelity. And perhaps the most insidious effect is that promiscuity can overshadow the real issue of what is actually happening—your spouse's depression—which trumps everything. The next section offers some helpful tools, but perhaps one of the most critical things you can do for yourself is to repeat, as many times as you need to, "This behavior is the illness, not my spouse."

FOR REFLECTION

How do I experience sexual expression beyond the act of intercourse?

What are my feelings about different sexual practices?

What sexual boundaries do my spouse and I need to discuss?

SURVIVING THE CHANGES

Sexual expression serves to deepen the marriage relationship, to bring a couple to an intense level of intimacy. When that expression is gone or takes on strange and threatening forms, trust can be shattered. In order to get through this tough time, there are several strategies that can help.

• Keep talking

As difficult as it might be to talk about the sexual changes in your marriage, it is important that you and your spouse talk about them. You need to acknowledge what is happening, to show your husband or wife that you are trying to understand. You need to be honest with your spouse about how you are feeling about the changes in your sexual relationship. It is especially important to acknowledge the strength and destructiveness of the depression in your sexual relationship.

If talking together as a couple is too difficult, it can be helpful to talk together with someone who can guide the conversation. Since feelings about sex are intensely personal, it can be difficult to look at the subject objectively. But in fighting the effects of depression it is sometimes necessary to put aside those concerns and talk openly and honestly, searching out ways together to have a healthier relationship. Finding someone who can help you talk through this delicate subject can make growth possible.

• Express love and care

It is important to continue to keep reassuring your spouse that you care, that there are others who care, and that you and they are willing to keep working through this illness. Also consider ways other than sex in which you can express your love for your spouse physically: a gentle touch, a foot rub at the end of the day, attentiveness to his or her conversation (despite the long ramblings to which some depressed individuals are prone). Look for ways beyond intercourse to have intimacy.

• Express your interest in sex

An extremely important fact to remember is that your partner's lack of interest in sex is not connected to your desirability. You are still a desirable individual. Continue to let your spouse know of your interest in sex. Don't avoid touching each other.

When intercourse is not possible because of the depth of a spouse's depression, some people consider satisfying their own sexual needs through masturbation. People have a wide range of feelings about self-gratification, based on their family background, religious beliefs and comfort level, but it can be a healthy way to satisfy one's sexual needs in this situation. Take time to consider how, or whether, this might be an alternative for you.

• Take care of yourself

When you are living with a depressed spouse, you are in a situation that can attack your self-esteem and the depth of your marriage relationship. In order not to follow this downward spiral, first and foremost, you will need to take care of yourself. If you're thinking, 'Everyone keeps saying that, but they don't really understand—there's just no time,' this next statement is for you: *Self-care is not a negotiable item.* You need to nurture yourself while you navigate these rough waters of depression. Taking time for yourself every day, whether you take a walk through your neighborhood, an evening at the movies or a long bath, is as much an important part of "treatment" as your spouse's medications.

FOR REFLECTION

What's my comfort level in discussing our sexual relationship with my spouse? How might we benefit from this discussion? Whom could we turn to for help in looking at our physical relationship more openly?

When do I feel undesirable? When do I feel desirable?

What do I need to do to nurture my own sexuality? What are my feelings about using masturbation to meet my sexual needs in this case?

How can I continue to physically express my love to my spouse?

THE GREAT LOVER

When depression affects sex in a marriage, it can wreak an incredible amount of destruction. The very intimacy of the union is threatened, and the non-depressed spouse is often left emotionally and physically bereft.

If this is how you are feeling, you may find yourself not only blaming your partner but also blaming God: "If God truly loved and cared about me, God wouldn't be allowing this to happen!" The catch is that if you close yourself off from intimacy with God you are denying yourself the very intimacy that will help you ride out this depression and grow closer to your spouse.

It's critically important to remember that, even in darkest times, God will not abandon you. The intimacy of the Great Lover is always there for you, despite how you may be feeling or what you may be thinking. This might be a good time to pray the prayer of the anguished father who brought his son to Jesus for healing: "I believe. Help my unbelief" (Mark 9:24).

FOR REFLECTION

What is my relationship with God at this time?

What does being intimate with God mean to me?

How can I remind myself daily of God's great love for me?

DEPRESSION'S EFFECT
ON FAITH

"My God, my God, why have you forsaken me?" (Mark 15:34).
These words of Jesus on the cross have been repeated many times by people who suffer from depression. Unable to see a way out of the deepening sadness and despair, they feel a great sense of abandonment and loneliness. This feeling is not limited to the depressed, however. Faith is often a casualty of depression both for the depressed and the non-depressed spouse. Depressive illness has the capacity to chip away at faith and block avenues of hope. Well spouses may have the same sense of abandonment and loneliness as their depressed partner, feeling that God is present for everyone but them.

"Some days are better than others. They flow according to how he is," says Mary, whose husband has been suffering from clinical depression for over a year. "I pray for him and for me, and how that helps or hinders depends on the day. Too often, though, I do feel abandoned by God, and I find I am seriously beginning to doubt my faith."

John's wife experienced severe depression following childbirth: "God was nowhere to be found. I prayed. I cried. I prayed some more, but God refused to answer me. It was so hard. I went through times when I couldn't believe, when I was angry with a God who seemed to not care. It is only in looking back that I can see God was with me the whole time."

Depression challenges faith in ways unimagined. It can cause doubt, anger, resignation and hatred. It can nurture cynicism and sarcasm and feelings of abandonment. People who feel abandoned by God may even fear punishment. Though they are told of a God who cares about them and wants the very best for them, life with a depressed spouse may leave them suddenly feeling as if their prayers go unanswered and that a loving God doesn't even exist. After all, if God were there, or if they believed enough, this depression would

93

be gone, wouldn't it? Feeling guilty about such thoughts, they fear punishment. Some abandon any pretense of hanging onto faith. They don't feel as if they can pray, let alone pray often enough or well enough in the "right" way.

Perhaps you have found yourself feeling or thinking some of these things. You are not alone. It might help to consider the fact that many people of faith have struggled with the effects of depression. Therese of Lisieux, the saint of the Little Way, often spoke of God's abandonment as she dealt with depression. Augustine wrestled with the illness, expressing it through his promiscuity. Martin Luther fought the grip of depression throughout his life, and also had the pain of watching his wife, Katie, live with severe anxiety. .

THE ENCOURAGEMENT OF SCRIPTURE

Throughout scripture there also are stories of men and women who dealt with depression. Job is perhaps the most known example. One catastrophe after another struck, leaving him feeling more and more abandoned by God. Depression became his bedfellow. But because Job trusted God he eventually found peace. King David wrestled with the demon of depression, many of his soulful Psalms being an expression of the depths of despair he felt. And yet these same Psalms speak of a love and intimacy with his Creator that helped David overcome his depression. Several of the people seeking Jesus obviously struggled with depression's hold: the woman at the well, the rich young man, Mary Magdala. These and so many others who encountered Jesus came with little hope, beaten down by life and the circumstances dealt them. Many of them, however, because of their willingness to be open to God, were transformed by God's love.

Scripture holds many words of encouragement. St. Paul wrote "by the encouragement of the scriptures we might have hope"

(Romans 15:4). He also referred to God as the "God of all consolation" (2 Corinthians 1:3). God's own words are a promise of caring: "As a mother comforts her child, so I will comfort you" (Isaiah 66:13).

Depression is a terrible illness. People afflicted with it, and those who love them, feel its tentacles around every aspect of their lives, every moment of their days. Family suffers; faith suffers. But in all that suffering, God is walking steadily with us, carrying us when we need to be carried, whispering words of support through the many blessings around us, extending a loving touch through the family of faith.

Even when everything seems to be falling apart, hold onto these words the psalmist wrote long ago:

> God is our refuge and strength, a very present help in trouble. Therefore we will not fear, though the earth should change, though the mountains shake in the heart of the sea; though its waters roar and foam, though the mountains tremble with its tumult. The Lord of hosts is with us; the God of Jacob is our refuge. (Psalm 46:1-3, 7)

FOR REFLECTION

What scripture verses or texts have been meaningful to me in the past?

What encouragement might they hold for me now?

Who are some saints or heroes I can cling to?

THE COMFORT OF PRAYER

"Because of my wife's depression, I get so busy trying to keep things together that I neglect time for prayer," says Michael. "It is at the bottom of my to-do list, but on reflection I know it should be at the very top."

When you're dealing with a depressed spouse, it's difficult to find time to pray formally. There is just too much to do. Managing kids, paying bills, handling all the tasks necessary for day-to-day life—it's demanding work, day in and day out. But prayer may be one of the most valuable things you can do on any given day.

Your prayer doesn't need to be polished or practiced or politically correct. You might choose to engage in formal prayers because you draw comfort from familiar words and routines. But if it helps, let go of traditional ideas of what prayer is supposed to look like. Someday there might be the time and energy for those traditional structures, but right now, being with God in some way is what matters.

If formal prayer is too difficult for you just now, try to recognize a different form of prayer. Make an effort to imagine God beside you each day in every task you do; drying the dishes while you're washing, navigating in the passenger seat while you're driving, holding your hand as you fall asleep. With God as part of your family, prayer becomes an everyday occurrence.

Consider, as well, setting aside a time each day, even if it's only five minutes, to be alone in prayer with your God. There are many ways to experience this prayer time. You may want to just be quiet before God, spending time in reflection, letting God take in your feelings, thoughts and frustrations. As Martin Luther so aptly put it, "The fewer the words, the better the prayer." You might want to hug yourself and imagine the comforting hands of God. Or you could sit and rock before God's watchful eyes. Your prayer time may have to be when everyone else is asleep, or maybe when you're in the shower.

Whatever form your prayer takes, this regular time can help you approach whatever is going on at home with a new outlook and sense of purpose. Prayer is an opportunity to nurture yourself in an environment that allows no time for nurture. Prayer can make a seemingly absent God real to you once again. And when you take the time to become quiet and know that God is God, other things become more manageable.

FOR REFLECTION
What forms of prayer are meaningful for me?

What times during my day would lend themselves to prayer time?

What form of prayer would fit for me right now?

THE PERSPECTIVE OF BLESSINGS
The lyrics of one of Bing Crosby's classic songs offered a simple solution for not being able to sleep: to count your blessings instead of sheep. That is good advice.

The difficulty of living with a depressed spouse can cloud your eyes and condition you to look only at what is wrong. But blessings still exist, even during depression, if you can open your eyes to them.

Therese has two children and a husband who has gone through two major depressions. She recalls, "My kids were five and ten at the time, old enough to know something was up but not old enough to know the enormity of it all. I knew it was important that I stay positive for them, so I started each day by listing my blessings. I have to admit that some days I only had one or two, but on other days, I found I had more than my share.

"On one of the particularly bad mornings, I was having trouble thinking of blessings because my husband had disappeared for a time the night before. I didn't know where he was until the police called. Even though he was all right, despite getting into an accident, I felt as if everything was going wrong.

"My son came up to me and asked what I was doing. I told him that I was trying to write my blessings that morning in my journal. He looked at the empty page and then at me.

"'Mom,' he said, 'I think you should put yourself at the top of the list this morning because, even though you look tired, you got up to get me breakfast and that makes you a blessing for you and for me.'

"My son blessed me that day. My page filled up quickly after that, and I realized that listing my blessings was a powerful, powerful tool."

"Count your blessings" may sound like a trite adage, but it truly can help you keep things in perspective. When you are dealing with a depressed spouse, it is easy to be pulled into the quagmire and to think that nothing will be right again. The actual act of recording your blessings can allow the positive aspects of your life to gain in strength. It can help you be more conscious of how God is working in your life, and that awareness will enable you to pull yourself through moments of doubt.

One way to get in the habit of counting your blessings is to take a few minutes at the end of each day to list at least three blessings. Some days these may be big, important things: healthy children, a warm home in a winter storm, a support system of family and friends. Other days it may be harder to find those positives. But even if your list consists of seemingly minute, mundane items—the baby took a long nap, your boss didn't yell at you, and you managed to get to the post office before it closed—making the effort to look on the bright side can make a difference. Depression makes it too easy to focus only on negatives. Sometimes it requires a conscious, intentional effort to move away from this tendency.

FOR REFLECTION

What blessings are occurring in my life, in spite of my spouse's illness?

What three blessings did I receive in the last day or so?

How can I intentionally keep these blessings before me so I won't keep focusing on the negatives in my life?

—

THE FAITHFULNESS OF GOD

As you walk through depression with your spouse—particularly when nothing seems to be working—God promises to be with you, to forgive any failings and mistakes and to give you peace. God will never abandon you. That is God's pact with you.

At times when you are feeling especially discouraged, when the demons of depressive illness seem particularly strong, these are good times to check the health of your PACT with God. Go back to pages 41-43 and re-read the description of a PACT. If you are keeping a journal, or have recorded your PACT with God in some way, re-read your promise. Even if you are not feeling close to God right now, or if you are wondering if God is even there, your PACT still holds. This is what makes a pact so valuable: It's a "through thick and thin, no matter what happens" kind of commitment, a pledge of loyalty and trust that nothing can break, not even your own lapses.

Any anger, frustration or feelings of failure you have are not evidence that God has left you to work through this alone. The God who knows how many hairs are on your head surely knows what you are feeling and wants to help. This might be a good time to remind yourself that God cherishes you at all times, despite how you may be feeling.

When John looked back on the time his wife suffered through depression, he was reminded of a song that came back to him whenever he was particularly stressed. It spoke of a merciful God who saves and keeps us safe despite darkness and fear: "I felt as if saying those words—that my God would indeed save us—would make my wife well again, would help our family grow. Looking back, I can see that God was carrying the whole family, helping us every step of the way. Looking back, all the puzzle pieces fit together, and the puzzle showed us the loving care of our God and deepened our faith."

FOR REFLECTION

What is my relationship with God at this point? How do I feel about this?

How might I be able to recognize and accept God's loving grace in this difficult time?

What part of my PACT with God needs strengthening? (See pages 41-43.)

People of Faith Who Struggled with Depression

Many people of faith have struggled with depression. As you read their words, keep in mind the gifts they shared and the beauty they brought to the world in spite of their personal struggles.

"Part of every misery is, so to speak, the misery's shadow or reflection: the fact that you don't merely suffer but have to keep on thinking about the fact that you suffer. I not only live each endless day in grief, but live each day thinking about living each day in grief."

—C. S. Lewis

"I am now the most miserable man living. If what I felt were distributed to the whole human family, there would not be one happy face on the earth. I must die or be better it appears to me. I awfully forbode I shall not."

—Abraham Lincoln

"In my soul I can't tell you how dark it is, how painful, how terrible. I feel like refusing God."

— Mother Teresa

"Again, joy in the Holy Ghost I have not. I have now and then some starts of joy in God, but it is not that joy for it is not abiding."

— John Wesley

"And now, O Lord, please take my life from me, for it is better for me to die than to live."

—Jonah (Jonah 4:3)

"Why did I come forth from the womb to see toil and sorrow, and spend my days in shame?"

—Jeremiah (Jeremiah 20:18)

THE CHALLENGES
OF TREATMENT

The obituary read, "After a gallant fight with depression, he finally succumbed to suicide. The young father is dead at the age of 39."

Despite the best of efforts, the use of medication, extensive therapy and supportive people, depression sometimes destroys. It destroys through suicide, through alcoholism, through other addictions, through divorce.

"I had so much faith in the medication. I was sure it was going to work. Each time I had hope, but then it didn't work for lots of different reasons," says Sam, whose wife has suffered from depression off and on throughout twenty years. "Right when we thought we had it conquered, the medicine would stop working. It was maddening."

FINDING THE RIGHT TREATMENT BALANCE

• Finding the right medication

Today medications abound for the treatment of depression. However, it is also a fact that the world of medicine still lacks a definitive way of diagnosing depression and determining what type of medication will work best.

"We go by different signs to determine depression," says Stephen Samuelson, a psychiatrist in Kansas City, Missouri. "With those signs we need consistency of appearance with at least five of the symptoms in order to have a diagnosis of depression. And even then it is difficult to determine what is causing the depression, which could be anything from outside events, such as a death in the family, to a serious brain chemical imbalance."

Finding the right medication is not easy. There is not one magic pill that works for everyone. Often it is a case of trial and error, combining medications to arrive at the proper dosage effective for the individual. "The doctors would prescribe one type of medication, and when it was clear that it wasn't working, we would have to wean my husband off of it and then start again," says Mary. "Usually it takes ten days to a month, and sometimes even longer, for a medication to click in. It is not an easy time. There is no quick fix in depression."

Then there is the problem of self-medication. Sometimes when depressed people begin to feel better, they decide on their own that medication is no longer necessary and discontinue it without consulting a doctor. This usually has disastrous results. Serious side effects can occur when antidepressants are stopped "cold turkey." And when antidepressants are stopped abruptly, it takes time to regain the therapeutic level that had been achieved to that point.

Sometimes psychiatrists will suggest cutting back, increasing or changing medication out of concern for over-medicating or under-medicating or because of damage to organs or for various other reasons. Such changes are often undertaken without consulting the non-depressed spouse, who is actually able to give the most accurate feedback on the medication and how it is or is not working. Sometimes the well spouse is left to pick up the pieces when medication fails due to changes made by doctors.

"I wish the psychiatrist had asked me my opinion," says Sally. "She still might have decided to cut the medication down for my husband, but at least I could have told her my observations, things that she didn't see on a day-to-day basis. I have deep anger about the fact that it was done and that I had to deal with the consequences."

As effective and essential as medications can be in the treatment of depression, it is not an easy road. It will require your patience and persistence—perhaps even some pushing to get your spouse to stay on track with the medications that are working.

• Finding the right therapist

Some depressed people find relief through medications alone. Others can improve through psychotherapy alone. However, the most effective treatment, according to the National Institute of Mental Health, is a combination of both antidepressant medication and therapy. But just as finding the best medication for a depressed person can be difficult, finding the right therapist can also be a complex process.

"There were therapists and there were therapists. Some just were not a good fit. Others said things that only made the situation worse," recalls Mary of the trek she and her husband took through the land of diagnosis and treatment. "When we finally found the right one, it made all the difference."

It may take several visits with a therapist to determine whether he or she is a good fit for your spouse. As the healthy spouse, you will probably need to take an active role in making this determination. You can ask gentle questions to find out how your spouse feels about the therapist and about his or her progress toward recovery. You might want to request permission from your spouse to discuss treatment with therapists and psychiatrists in order to share your perspective on progress or lack thereof. You may even need to make decisions regarding the treatment of your spouse.

"I remember we searched and searched for a therapist," says Joe of his thirteen-year bout with depression. "We found someone who seemed to be helpful, and then he started in on the pulling-yourself-up-by-your-bootstraps scenario and we knew he was no longer the right one for us. Actually, I should say that my wife knew he wasn't the right one for us because, at that point in time, I was not able to make any real decisions about anything. I had trouble even deciding what pair of socks to wear for the day."

If therapy with a particular therapist is not helping, it is important to acknowledge this and look elsewhere. Trusting your instincts and monitoring the progress of treatment are essential in making the best use of your counseling options. Remember that you and your spouse are the ones shopping for a professional who can help in the treatment of this illness. You have the right to choose someone who will be best for your loved one and best for you. Therapy can be a huge step toward recovery, but only if the therapist is one who works well with both of you.

Guidelines for Finding the Right Therapist

- Ask for referrals from people you trust: physicians, ministers, family, friends.

- If an accurate diagnosis has already been made, look for a therapist who specializes in that diagnosis.

- Different therapists use different approaches. Some will focus on finding root causes for problems, others will work mainly on making practical behavioral changes, others may use a combination of approaches. Consider which route is likely to be most helpful for you and your spouse.

- Look for a therapist who is open to inviting you, the well spouse, to some sessions. You have a huge stake in your spouse's recovery, and your feedback and concerns should be heard.

- Allow a fair amount of time with a therapist before making a decision about whether he or she is the right "fit." It can take several sessions to build a relationship before progress can even begin to be made. On the other hand, pay attention to your own instincts and your spouse's reactions to the therapist. If they aren't "clicking," don't be afraid to suggest that it's time to look elsewhere.

• Seeking alternative treatments

Sometimes when the usual treatments just do not work, someone along the way may recommend electroconvulsive therapy (ECT). ECT was long considered an archaic and barbaric treatment for mental illness. But with major advances in understanding the brain, physicians today are able to use ECT as a useful tool in treating severe depression. This treatment gives electromagnetic shock to the brain through brief, generalized, controlled seizures that cause a change in the neurotransmitters. ECT may stop depression for up to six months and beyond, especially when used with anti-depressants. However, the patient can suffer from short-term memory loss and must be monitored for several days.

Some individuals turn to herbal treatments, such as St. John's Wort. Others may look to spiritualists to help them. Some depressed persons do nothing and assume that God will cure them. Searching for the best treatment for your loved one can be an unpredictable venture. What works for one person does not always work for another. But if there is one known fact among all these unknowns, it is this: Depression, when left alone, can go to depths that make it nearly impossible for the individual to surface again. So keep seeking, keep trying and keep trusting God.

FOR REFLECTION

How willing am I to talk with my spouse about how treatment is going? How can I benefit from facilitating my spouse's treatment?

How willing am I to question my spouse's therapist and discuss my spouse's progress?

What positive results am I seeing due to my spouse's treatment? What negative results am I seeing?

WHEN TREATMENTS DON'T WORK

Sometimes, despite everyone's best efforts, depression simply does not lift. Perhaps your spouse is finding no relief from medication, no matter what mixture of prescriptions are tried. Sometimes, no matter what courses of action you take, things do not work out. The pain for either you or your spouse may become too much.

• Facing the end of a marriage

If your spouse's depression has deepened, the relationship that perhaps for years has given you an emotional closeness and dependability may no longer be there. Your relationship may have changed into that of a parent and child. Or you and your spouse may have become adversaries, always at odds with one another. Arguments between the two of you may have begun to bring out anger and even violence, and you and your children might be living in fear of what could happen next. Alcohol, drug abuse, sexual addiction and physical abuse can become a depressed person's way of operating, and the effects can take a heavy toll on the rest of the family. Both you and your spouse may be physically and emotionally spent and see no way out.

"When I finally realized that no matter what I said, or how much I pleaded, he wasn't going to listen; when I realized he wasn't really a parent anymore; when all interactions between him and me and between him and the kids were negative; when I found myself very short with the kids, even spanking them, I knew I had to do something," recalls Anna. "But it was still another six months before I filed for divorce. It was a really hard decision to make. I hate to say that divorce is the answer in any marriage, but if you've done everything you can for the depressed person and absolutely nothing helps…."

Sometimes, as much as you would like to think that your marriage will survive, circumstances of safety and growth make divorce or legal separation a necessary move. If you have begun to see your children suffer from the negative choices made by the depressed parent, divorce or legal separation may be the safest alternative. While some religions oppose divorce generally as an overly simple solution to marital problems, all of them respect the right of an abused spouse to leave a dangerous situation.

Though you made marriage vows before God, you also need to remember that God wants only the best for both you and your spouse and your children. Sometimes ending a marriage is the only choice left for all concerned.

• Dealing with suicidal thoughts

When therapy, medication or other alternatives do not work, the possibility of committing suicide may move more into prominence for the depressed spouse. The subject of suicide should never be treated lightly. When things are not going well in treatment, it is important to explore with your depressed spouse any feelings and thoughts he or she might have about such an action. Ask directly: "Do you feel that suicide is a possible option? Have you envisioned a specific suicide scenario?"

Don't be afraid to talk about it. Bringing up the subject of suicide does not increase the likelihood of it happening. As with all other aspects of this illness, openness is the healthiest course of action.

When depression is present and suicide has become a possibility, it is important that you form a pact of protection with your depressed spouse, particularly if he or she is thinking of executing the idea. Often called a "no-suicide contract," this basically is an agreement in which your spouse promises not to hurt himself or herself and includes contingency plans if he or she feels in danger of doing so. The contract can be renegotiated or renewed as needed and can be merely verbal, but it is often more effective if you and your spouse write out a simple agreement. Here is one sample:

No-Suicide Contract

I,_____, promise that I will not attempt to harm myself in any way or attempt suicide.

If I feel suicidal, I will remind myself that I have promised not to harm myself, under any circumstances, in any way.

If I feel in immediate danger of hurting myself, I will call 911 or go to the nearest emergency room.

If I am having suicidal thoughts, I will call the following people until I reach one of them and tell them what is happening to me: (Insert names and phone numbers of those to be called, in priority order.)

Signed: _____

Witnessed: _____

The bottom line is to get your spouse to talk to you (or someone he or she trusts) before doing anything. Get into the habit of inquiring, "Is it safe to leave you alone today?" Keeping thoughts and feelings out in the open is an important way to keep life from looking so miserable that death looks like a welcome alternative. Having a pact of protection may keep your spouse alive.

• Dealing with suicide

In the worst-case scenario, suicide may be the fatal outcome of an illness that has already stripped so much from a family. Sometimes, despite what avenues have been tried, no matter how supportive the family has been, the pain is too great and the depressed person chooses to end the pain by ending his or her life.

When suicide takes place, those left behind may find themselves wondering, "What could I have done? How did I miss the signs? If only I had been a better spouse, this wouldn't have happened." The list of questions and recriminations could go on and on, but this kind of reaction doesn't serve a helpful purpose.

When a person dies of cancer or a heart attack, would we ask, "What could I have done to stop the disease? What if I had paid more attention to her? What if I hadn't taken the new job?" No, we don't ask those questions because we know that sometimes death is the end result of cancer or heart disease or other factors beyond our control. It is the same with depression.

Depression and Suicide

Fifteen percent of people with depression commit suicide. (National Health Care Quality Report, 2003)

The strongest risk factors for attempted suicide in adults are depression, alcohol abuse, cocaine use, and separation or divorce. (National Institute of Mental Health)

Four times as many men as women commit suicide, but more women than men report a history of attempted suicide, with a gender ratio of 3 to 1. (National Institute of Mental Health)

Suicide is the eleventh leading cause of death in the United States. (National Institute of Mental Health)

If you have experienced the tragedy of suicide, it is not helpful to continually raise questions about what you should or should not have done. Suicide sometimes claims a victim despite all the good intentions of doctors and families—even the depressed person. It is a sad fact that cannot be disputed. The more pressing question is, how in the midst of all this, can you take care of yourself? How can you survive and keep growing?

FOR REFLECTION

Based on what's happening in our relationship, is it time for me to consider ending the marriage? What feelings arise when I consider this possibility?

If my spouse has considered suicide, what pact of protection do I need to secure with him or her?

If suicide should occur, what plans do I have in place to protect my own mental and emotional health and that of our children?

IN THE AFTERMATH

If treatment for your spouse's depression has failed and you find yourself facing divorce or your spouse's suicide, first and foremost it is important to acknowledge the toll your emotions are taking—and will continue to take—on you. You may feel lonely, isolated, angry, hopeless, in pain—even depressed yourself. When any of this happens, it is important to seek help, whether through therapy, discussions with someone you trust or the care of a good friend or family member. You will need to nurture yourself emotionally during this tough time.

• Share your suffering

One of the best ways to nurture yourself is to talk out the situation with people you trust. Let everything out with someone with whom you feel safe. Give them the gift of sharing your suffering. Also, become aware of those around you who are lending support in small ways, even if it's something as simple as the grocery person who notices you when you go through the checkout line or your neighbor who brings a meal to you each week. You might want to make a list of these people and read the list every day on waking and on going to sleep. This is the chain of people who can give you some of the sustenance that once was available from your spouse.

• Refocus your thoughts

Refocusing is another way in which you can nurture yourself. Every time you find yourself thinking, "Poor me," see if you can shift your thinking to thoughts of "How blessed I am." Although you certainly do need to acknowledge your feelings of bereavement, you don't need to focus all your thoughts on them. Look around and notice the small ways in which you are blessed—by the sun, by a good friend, by a bowl of hot soup. Such seemingly small things can be important. Life *is* good and worth living. Deep down you know that.

• Laugh whenever you can

Laughter is like changing a diaper: You know it won't change anything permanently, but it will make everything okay for a while. That in and of itself can be a lifesaver. Look for things that will make you laugh. Choose to be with people who like to laugh. Make light of your own behavior. Look for silliness in the world around you. You might be surprised at the physical effect laughter has, even if you don't "feel" like laughing.

• Shift your anger to the illness

If you're feeling angry, focus your anger on the illness that robbed you and your spouse of the joy of life. Some have found it helpful to create a visual reminder that it is the depression that has changed things. Here's one exercise you might want to try: Place a photo of your spouse on a sheet of paper and surround it with words describing his or her good qualities. On another sheet, print the word *DEPRESSION* and surround the word with all the negative things you have experienced. Use this visual cue to remind you that it is the *illness*, not you or your spouse, that is responsible for the hurt in your life.

• Make a pact of protection with yourself

Pacts of protection are important not only for depressed people, but also for the well spouse. If you've experienced the sorrow of a loved one's suicide, you are especially vulnerable. Make a pact with yourself to seek out support from a specific list of individuals. Make a list of ways to care for yourself, and then actually do them. Refer to your list often so that you know what you can do to maintain your sanity during these trying times.

FOR REFLECTION

How willing am I to make the mind shift from negative to positive thinking? In what ways am I still blessed?

To what extent am I able to refocus my anger from my spouse to the illness?

To whom can I turn to for support? What will I include in my pact of protection for myself?

THE IMPORTANCE
OF SELF-CARE

When you live in close contact with a person suffering from depression, it can be surprising how easily that depression seems to become "contagious." Even when you have the best intentions of separating yourself from the illness—staying in control and remaining positive—the symptoms of depression can begin to show up in your own behavior. It's hard to keep smiling when you're faced with persistent frowns or tears.

And yet if you're the well spouse in the partnership, you know how vital it is to keep going. You are probably carrying the responsibility for keeping home, family and life together, and you may be needed to take the lead in helping your spouse find effective treatment. If you fall prey to the same illness, chaos is right around the corner.

It's important to keep in mind that depression can be situational. In other words, life events that cause severe distress can trigger a major depressive episode that requires the intervention of medication and/or therapy. No matter what the root cause of your spouse's illness, there is the very real possibility that the situation you find yourself in can trigger your own situational depression. This possibility underscores how important it is to care for yourself in this difficult time, monitor your own state of mental health and get help as you need it.

In the myriad of tasks and emotions you struggle through as the spouse of a depressed person, it's all too easy to let self-care fall to the wayside. It takes intentionality, but you owe it to yourself, your children and your spouse to do what you need to do to keep yourself healthy.

THE TRUTH WILL SET YOU FREE

It can't be stressed enough: Keeping your pain to yourself, trying to hide this illness from family and friends, will only multiply your problems. Openness about your needs and your fears can help you begin to deal with them.

As you share your situation with others, it's important to remember to frame depression in terms of an illness: It's a sickness that no one wants, that has attacked a loved one and is affecting the whole family. It's no different from cancer or diabetes or leukemia: It's an invasive, debilitating condition that requires both medical treatment and a strong support system in order to survive.

One especially difficult hurdle often faced by spouses of depressed people is how and whether to be open about the situation with new people. Casual acquaintants met at parties, new co-workers, new friends—all can present challenges as you decide how much to disclose. It's a delicate balance between a desire to start a new relationship with honesty and knowing when to put up protective boundaries.

Obviously, it's not appropriate in all situations to share the difficulties you're dealing with. It can be helpful to consider ahead of time what you're willing to share, even to the point of creating a mental script: "This is what I will share in this given situation, but in this other situation, I will share only this."

Your ability to read people will come into play at these times. Some of us have better instincts than others when it comes to first impressions. If you've found yourself able to accurately read first impressions in the past, trust your decisions about which new acquaintances are "safe" to share with. If, on the other hand, you doubt your ability to gauge new people, come down on the side of reticence: Wait and see how things develop.

As you weather the storm of depression, it's also important for you to continue being honest both with yourself and with your loving Creator. Keep sharing your pain with God. Lay out your anger, frustrations and fears. Allow God to help you see these feelings for what they are and accept them in yourself. This can go a long way toward helping you live with your feelings, deal with the depression and continue to move toward healing.

FOR REFLECTION

How am I feeling about what is happening to me, my spouse and my family as a result of my spouse's depression? How honest am I being with myself? With God?

To what extent have I shared my troubles with my closest family and friends? How could I benefit from being more open?

How comfortable am I with sharing my situation with new friends and acquaintances? What will I say to them about my spouse's depression?

WELL-BEING CHECKS

Because depression develops so easily and insidiously, it's important that you, as the healthy spouse in the partnership, check in on your own well-being. You need to think consciously about how you're reacting and feeling, and be aware of any warning signs that may signal you're not doing well emotionally.

Keeping a journal can be a useful tool for monitoring your emotional state. If journaling sounds like a daunting task, keep in mind that you can journal any way you like. A formal narrative of feelings, events and your reactions is one way to go about it. But simple one-word lists can also be effective. Stream-of-consciousness writing, without concern about word choice, sentences or even coherence, can be a good way to clear your mind and release some of your stress.

However you choose to keep track of your feelings, take a few minutes once a week or so to look over your thoughts and feelings for the past week. Do you see any trends? As you look back, you might discover ways that you were able to keep yourself going and be able to apply these in the future. Do your emotions or your ability to function seem to be taking a dive? If you notice a consistent downturn of coping abilities over several weeks, this may be a signal that you could benefit from therapy or consultation with a doctor yourself. If coming up with three blessings each day is becoming more difficult or impossible, that can be a red flag. It might be time to get serious about the importance of self-care and outside help.

FOR REFLECTION

What would be the most comfortable and helpful way for me to continually check in with how I'm feeling and coping?

What downward trends, if any, do I notice in my feelings? What do I want to do about that?

Do I feel I need outside help for myself?

LETTING GO OF GUILT

It crosses everyone's mind: If only I hadn't done that, this wouldn't have happened. If I had been more affirming, my spouse wouldn't be so depressed. If I would just get these things done, everything will be back to normal. We all have times when we think that if we had just done something differently, depression would not be on our doorstep.

If there is one message about depression that needs to be repeated again and again, it is this: You cannot stop depression by doing or not doing something. Depression happens regardless of what is going on around an individual. And it doesn't help to feed your spouse's depression with your own feelings of guilt.

Sometimes guilt feelings arise because you don't feel as if you can do all the same things you could "before." You may feel unable to serve others, to give your time at church—or even attend church. If you're feeling guilty, you might need a reality check: Living with a depressed spouse is exhausting. If you make the effort to get up and go to church, for example, but the result is crying children, an over-tired body and a fretful, agitated spouse, you have lost sight of what is important.

What is important is to present a whole person to God and to nurture that whole person. If that means sleeping in on a Sunday because you have been up with a sick child or stayed up late the night before to listen to your depressed spouse, let go of your guilt for not going to church. If someone asks you to fix a meal for a sick parishioner, and you simply are too exhausted, it's okay to say "no." In fact, it's okay to let others know that you are the one who needs a meal brought in.

Feelings of guilt can also arise when we feel we've failed our spouse, our children or ourselves. Perhaps you reacted with anger and sarcasm when your spouse slept all day and missed an important appointment. Maybe you were too tired to play with the children. Or maybe you didn't make time for prayer today. Because you are already feeling overburdened, guilt and anxiety may set in. Do your best to remember these points:

- You are a fragile human being, doing your best under very difficult circumstances.

- You may have made a mistake. But we all make mistakes—every day. None of us gets it right all the time.

- God is beside you through every mistake, loving you, forgiving you and affording you the grace to try again and again and again.

- Guilt will not help you move on. Guilt will only make everything harder. Accept God's forgiveness and do your best to forgive yourself and move on.

- God calls you to love others as you love yourself. Rejecting feelings of guilt is a way to love yourself.

FOR REFLECTION

What do I feel guilty about?

What could I do to let go of that guilt?

What could I do to nurture myself instead?

SEEKING HELP FOR YOURSELF

If the burden of living with a depressed spouse becomes too heavy to bear alone, consider counseling for yourself. Ask friends or your physician for help finding a good therapist, or visit with a minister if that's comfortable for you. Perhaps there is a Stephen Ministry program in your area. This is an ecumenical ministry that provides one-on-one Christian caring for those who are hurting due to life's challenges. While Stephen Ministers are not licensed counselors, they are trained to listen, to pray with those in pain, to help hurting people maintain and expand their relationship with God, and to help with referrals to licensed professionals when a need for deeper assistance is indicated.

"I wasn't sure at first how a Stephen Minister could help me deal with my wife's depression," says George. "I knew they weren't supposed to even try to solve problems. But when I met with the man, I was able to get a lot of stuff off my chest. He didn't judge, didn't try to fix things; he just listened. That did help. It also helped that he was a person of faith. Then, too, he noticed when I showed signs of being near the edge myself, and he suggested I get professional help. I took his advice."

Many churches will be willing and able to help you find where and how to get connected to a Stephen Minister. Most congregations do not require that those receiving care from a Stephen Minister be members of their community.

Whether you seek help for yourself through a mental health professional, a Stephen Minister or some other source, you are likely to benefit from the perspective of someone who's been trained to listen objectively. Remember, self-care is not optional for the spouse of a depressed person, and counseling can be an excellent way to care for yourself.

FOR REFLECTION

With whom, beyond my friends and family, do I need to talk?

Who might I approach for guidance?

Do I need professional counseling for myself?

MAINTAINING "NORMAL"

As a spouse of a depressed person, there may be times when things get so out of hand that you forget what "normal" looks like. Keeping your routines and schedules as normal as possible can go a long way in helping you make it through each day. A specified time for meals, a Bible study group you've been attending, a regularly scheduled time to do laundry or buy groceries, even a daily shower—all these routines can help you feel that life isn't out of control.

Your spouse's illness, however, may affect your ability to maintain your routines. He or she may feel unable to follow through with tasks or unable to keep any schedule consistently. When you're ready to leave for the dinner party that's been on the calendar for weeks, for example, you might find your spouse sitting in front of the television, trying to gather the energy to shower and dress to go with you.

For several reasons, it can be helpful for you to continue attending events and arriving at them punctually, even when your spouse cannot. Waiting around for your spouse to get ready and get out the door can result in anger, frustration and embarrassment as you arrive at your destination late. You're already struggling with a great many emotions, and this is one situation you can take control of and avoid.

Going ahead with your plans can benefit your spouse as well. "I couldn't count the times I hauled our three small children to church on my own," says Sarah. "Sometimes Brad would get himself there in time for the sermon, but sometimes he didn't make it at all. I missed sharing worship time with him, and it was always hard to manage the three kids on my own, but I knew I would feel worse if I missed church. Then, too, we were late for every event we tried to go to. I would wander around the house, steaming, ready to explode; I can't stand running late. One night I finally went to a party by myself, leaving early enough to get there on time, and left Brad to come if and when he could manage it. He arrived about an hour later. It turned out to be a breakthrough for both of us. I had the fun of being with friends and the satisfaction of arriving on time, and I was also able to avoid the anger I would have felt if I'd waited around for him. For his part, Brad was able to get himself ready at his own pace, without worrying how his lethargy was affecting me. He was actually glad I'd gone ahead without him."

Following through with plans and routines can have another positive effect. By observing you carrying on with your life, your spouse may be able to see that whenever he or she is able to return to health and a "normal" life, it will still be there.

FOR REFLECTION

What routines have I stopped? What do I miss?

What routines would I like to add back into my life?

How might this help both me and my spouse?

A PLACE FOR PAMPERING

For some, the word "pampering" conjures up images of spoiled rich people who are self-indulgent to the extreme. But pampering doesn't have to mean expensive dinners, pedicures and massages (although if any of these helps and you can afford it, there's nothing wrong with this type of pampering). The kind of pampering we are talking about is a nurturing form of self-care in small doses—any small pleasure that can help you relax. Think of a "treat" for yourself as a way to "treat" what ails you. It can make a big difference in your ability to survive life with a depressed spouse.

Pampering doesn't have to take a great deal of time, planning or expense, but it does mean being mindful of your need for a break, your need to do a little something just for your own pleasure. Relaxation, even for a short time, can energize you so you can go back to dealing with the day's problems.

• Get moving

Exercise is a great way to deal with stress. Not only does it distract you from your troubles, but it releases endorphins that are crucial to mood elevation. And you don't need an expensive gym membership to do it. A brisk walk with a stroller, a twenty-minute aerobic session with a DVD, or an extended dancing session in the living room with preschoolers—all are legitimate and productive forms of exercise.

• The great escape

Escapes of any kind are another good way to relax. It doesn't have to be huge to be helpful. You might escape into a good novel, or rent a movie you've always wanted to see, and get lost in the story. Even if you have to watch or read in short bursts between household tasks, while waiting for your spouse at a therapy appointment, or in the twenty minutes before you drop from exhaustion in the evening, it will be time well-spent. Forgetting about your own story for a short time and immersing yourself in the story of a fictional character can be a great survival tool.

At other times, you many need a more substantial escape, where you can be yourself for a time rather than someone's parent. As much as you love your children and enjoy being with them, a period away from them will give you time to think, attend to tasks you can't do while parenting and regain your patience so you can get back in there and parent some more. Find someone to watch the kids occasionally and plan a get-away. If finances are strained, check out area retreat centers. Or perhaps friends who will be out-of-town for a weekend will let you take advantage of their quiet space.

Spending time with friends can also be a very helpful way to relax and re-energize. There may be times when you need to unload to a close friend. Dumping your negative emotions in the presence of someone outside the home who loves you can help you return to your depressed spouse with a more constructive attitude.

But the opposite may be true as well. Sometimes you may want to spend time with friends without talking about your situation at home. You might need to say, "I appreciate your concern, but tonight I don't feel like talking about depression. Let's just have fun." Good old-fashioned fun can also help you keep going.

"At one point," says Gina, "I had to ask a friend at church not to talk to me about my husband's depression and our situation. I knew she had the best of intentions, but I finally told her that if she wanted to help me she shouldn't bring it up unless I initiated it. There were many other people at church—loving, caring people who constantly asked how I was doing—to whom I never was able to say this, though. My church was no longer a haven for me."

Your children, too, can benefit from time away. They, too, suffer from the stress of living with a depressed person. Getting away from your family stress can help them keep going. Spending time with other families, families who aren't dealing with depression, can also help them gain a better perspective on life. They can see that all families are different and perhaps benefit from observing a healthier family environment.

• Time with God
Finally, an extremely important way to relax and re-energize is to make

time regularly to be alone with God. That time might be early in the morning before anyone else is awake. It might be on Sunday mornings when you can put the kids in the church nursery or in Sunday school so you can spend a few minutes in a prayer chapel. Or your time with God may be in a restroom stall at work after lunch break. God doesn't care when or how. God is always near, patiently waiting for you to cry out, listen and be comforted. Even if you begin to fear that God doesn't care, God will always hold you in love. When you make the time to feel and accept that love, you can gain strength to keep going.

FOR REFLECTION

How can I reasonably pamper myself with some exercise, rest and relaxation?

How can I have some fun?

How can I make time to be alone with God and experience God's presence?

THE CHALLENGES
OF RECOVERY

—

You will forget your misery; you will remember it as waters that have passed away. And your life will be brighter than the noonday; its darkness will be like the morning. And you will have confidence, because there is hope; you will be protected and take your rest in safety. (Job 11:16-18)

—

Spouses can and often do overcome depression. Though it may require a long period of time and a wide array of doctors, medications and therapy sessions, depression can be controlled. Recent statistics show that eighty percent of people who seek treatment for depression find relief. Recovery can feel like the receding of suffocating flood waters or the return of morning after a long period of darkness.

THE RETURN

The latest medicine has been in his system for three weeks. Finally, he's showing improvement. He gets out of bed before the kids leave for school. He shows an interest in his appearance, his children, his friends, you. His energy level is doubled, even tripled. Because the chemicals in his brain are finally beginning to balance out, therapy becomes more productive.

As you see your spouse come alive again, you start to notice changes. As she begins to feel more like herself, she takes up responsibilities—bill paying, sharing household chores, parenting tasks and decisions—that you've had to shoulder alone for so long. You find yourself with more free time: time to play with the kids, go out with friends, occasionally put yourself first for a change. Your stress level decreases, and you find you can take time to relax.

When you see your spouse return to you from depression, you

may feel that you're experiencing the return of an old friend. With a return to health, your partner, helpmate and lover comes back to you. Sharing events and feelings, laughing together about something you overheard at work, catching each other's eye across a noisy dinner table—these simple blessings return, and they are all the more precious after their absence.

"In the very worst days of Brad's illness," says Sarah, "I felt so lonely. I had girlfriends, but my husband was truly my best friend. I tried to tell him how much I missed him, but he was so distant it was as if he had moved away. His response was that I shouldn't even try to talk to him any more. He said he couldn't be there for me. I was devastated.

"After a very long time, Brad finally started to get better and act like himself again. I remember one day I came home feeling rotten because of something that had happened at work. He noticed, asked me what was wrong and listened to my story for the first time in many months. I cried buckets—not because of my rotten day, but because my best friend had finally come back."

With a return of this friend and partner may also come the return of romance. Romantic love is fed by the little glances, incidental touches and shared laughter that are often missing during depression. As your depressed spouse is able to look beyond himself or herself again and think of you, this aspect of your marriage may well blossom anew. This in turn may lead to a better, more satisfying, healthier sexual relationship than you experienced during the depression. Communication during this time is key. Talking gently and constructively about your feelings about sex can only improve your relationship. And knowing that you are still sexually attracted to each other can help your relationship continue on the road to recovery.

You may feel so relieved that your loved one has begun to improve that you are ready to rejoice and celebrate, thinking only of how wonderful it is that life can now return to normal. This is an understandable reaction—who wouldn't rejoice when such a crippling illness fades? What you may not realize, however, is that not only are there positive results when depression subsides but also there are definite challenges ahead.

Recovery from depression can be very much an up-and-down experience. Even as you see your spouse come alive again, even as you welcome the changes, new problems or concerns may also arise. It is important to know that the recovery process is different for each person and each couple. What you choose to do during the recovery period will be unique to your situation.

FOR REFLECTION

What positive changes am I seeing in my spouse?

What changes are happening in my life as a result of my spouse's improvement?

How do I feel about any changes in our sex life?

NAVIGATING THE CHANGES

• Changes in the marriage

When a marriage shifts from two functional, healthy adults to one who's functional and one who's depressed, there is a distinct change in the personality of the marriage. Power shifts to the healthy partner as the depressed spouse loses the energy to act and the ability to make decisions. New patterns begin to form in which the healthy spouse learns to take over and act alone.

When the depressed spouse begins to return to health, however, the kaleidoscope shifts yet again. With more energy, more interest in life, better concentration and ability to make decisions, the formerly depressed spouse may wish to resume partnership in the everyday aspects of family life. The patterns that helped you survive during the illness will need to be shifted to reflect your spouse's re-found interest in handling responsibilities. And though you may be incredibly relieved to be able to hand off some of the burden, changing those interim patterns isn't always easy.

"Trust was a big thing," says Sam about the time after his wife began to heal. "I had been burned so many times during the depression that I found I couldn't trust this new behavior. I knew in my heart I should, but it was so hard. The only thing that saved us was that I talked about it with her. I laid it on the line, and then it became easier to take that leap of trust."

The ways in which you and your spouse related during the illness probably won't feel comfortable during recovery. But the ways you related prior to the illness may not feel comfortable, either. In some ways, your formerly depressed spouse may be a whole new person, having learned things through the experience of depression and therapy that may have given him or her a very different outlook on life than before.

"I remember I was so afraid of being left behind," says Therese. "Here was this man who had grown through therapy, who had struggled with a life-threatening disease, who now loved life. He was like a new person. I didn't know how to relate and, besides, I was tired from having to do everything myself for so long."

Watching a spouse emerge from depression a "new" person, you might have a sense of feeling left behind. You're faced with someone who is growing and blossoming, right at a time when you've spent a memorable period of your life doing the job of two adults, just to keep your family going. Your spouse may feel re-energized, but you may feel exhausted. It's important to be aware of these feelings and discuss them together.

FOR REFLECTION

Now that my spouse is recovering, what changes am I seeing in our relationship?

How hard is it for me to give back some of the decision making and power in our marriage?

To what extent am I able to allow my spouse to be a full partner again?

How is my spouse's emerging energy affecting my own emotional life?

• Changes in parenting

Patterns of parenting are likely to experience a shift as a result of recovery as well. After being the parent in charge for a period of time, it can be difficult to remember that you have a partner to turn to once again. While it may be hard to let go of the control you've assumed over parenting concerns, seeing the return of a parenting partner can have great benefits, if you make the effort to appreciate it.

"Brad had been steadily improving for some time," says Sarah, "but it took a while for that fact to sink in with me. At one point I found myself worrying constantly about a situation with our older daughter. It was weeks before it occurred to me that our daughter had a father who now would not only be interested in her problems but might very well have some insights or suggestions I hadn't thought of. When I finally took my concern to Brad and we shared the weight of it, it was a shock to me to realize I wasn't a single parent any more. But it was a good shock!"

FOR REFLECTION

To what extent am I beginning to share parenting responsibilities again with my spouse? How am I feeling about this situation?

In what ways can I help my spouse in this transition?

What changes might I need to make now in my parenting?

• Changes for your children

A return to a two-healthy-parent family can also be a difficult adjustment for children. If they've had to get used to dealing exclusively with Dad for everything from lunch money to permission for dates to advice about problems at school, it can be very hard for them to learn to turn to Mom again. They may have learned the hard way that Mom was unavailable or unreliable for a time, and it may require intentional effort to unlearn this lesson.

As always, communication is vital. Talk openly with your children, at an appropriate level, about what their parent's return to health means. Remind them gently that they now have two parents they can turn to. "I know Mom wasn't well for a long time, but she's doing much better now. She would love to help you with this problem." This type of statement may have to be repeated many times, in many ways, before it becomes natural for them to turn to Mom again.

Accepting discipline from a formerly "absent" parent can also be a challenge for children. Again, gentle reminders of the parent's return to health and return to parenting can be helpful. You can also facilitate your spouse's authority by modeling. "Coming home late for supper is against the rules in this house. Your mother and I will discuss the consequences, and later you can ask her what you need to do to make up for it." As you consistently affirm the authority of the formerly depressed parent, you will be helping your children accept this return to a two-parent family.

FOR REFLECTION

How can I help our children turn to *both* parents now?

How are our children responding to a more healthy family life?

How am I responding to these changes?

—

THE IMPORTANCE OF CHECK-INS

When you begin to see improvement in your spouse, it's tempting to push for an immediate and complete return to normal life: "She's feeling better; she should start looking for a job;" or "he should be caring for the kids again; he needs to get back to her routine."

But as with any illness, recovery is a process—sometimes a long and unpredictable one. Depression can change course, requiring new or different treatments, and it is often a chronic illness that requires constant monitoring. While letting go of some of the burdens that have been placed on you, you will still need to monitor your spouse's emotional health.

For example, handing back too much responsibility too quickly can backfire. This is a time when communication is key. Now that your spouse is more able to handle serious conversations, check in regularly about how much responsibility he or she is feeling able to take back. A scheduled check-in time—whether it's a weekly dinner, coffee in the afternoon, or a daily e-mail—can be very beneficial in maintaining communication. Ask specific questions: "Bill-paying day is tomorrow; do you feel like you can tackle that?" or "We need to make a decision about the repairs on the car; how are you feeling about that decision?" Be available to step in and take over if your spouse starts to become overwhelmed. Now that your spouse is in recovery, you can be hopeful that a period of feeling overwhelmed won't last forever.

Journaling can help you keep track of how things are going during the recovery period. If a written journal doesn't work for you, consider making a voice recording of your observations. Take note of your spouse's sleep patterns and "grouchy" episodes. Record any symptoms that have been especially notable, so you can look back over a period of time and watch for trends. Note any correlation between medication changes and behavior. Whether you see improvement that can be celebrated and appreciated, or whether you see downward spirals that need to be addressed with doctors and therapists, your observations will go a long way toward maintaining perspective and helping both of you see where you stand. This intentional approach can also help you retain a healthy sense of control over the recovery process.

It's also important not to overreact to situations that may, at first glance, appear to signal a return to depression. After battling depression for a long period, it is common for the well spouse to become suspicious and skeptical. Yes, your spouse is making progress. You see major changes for the better in many aspects of life. But you've been badly hurt by the illness that invaded your lives, and you're constantly fearful of its return.

"I became hyper," says Sam. "Once I saw something that even hinted of depression, I was on her case. Was she all right? Did she need to see the doctor? Was she taking her medicine? Poor gal! She wasn't able to have the normal up and down moods we all have. I wanted her to be 'up' all the time if she were truly well, and none of us can do that."

One day of grouchiness may well have a simple root cause. For example, it could be that your spouse just had a rotten day at work. Indecision over how to pay for a certain bill doesn't necessarily mean your spouse is on a downward spiral; maybe he or she is just coming down with a cold and is feeling "fuzzy." As Freud so famously put it, "Sometimes a cigar is just a cigar." Remember that if depression has returned you'll notice a number of these negative behaviors over a longer period of time. Try not to jump to a conclusion; just wait and observe.

Overreacting to what could simply be normal moodiness can create a two-fold problem. You may experience fear that can cause you to return to your old patterns: "I'd better take back all control before things get crazy around here again." And your spouse's recovery can be sabotaged: "I must be incapable of truly improving, since my spouse is still so sure I'm depressed." If you're not careful, the relationship patterns that may have finally started to shift back toward a healthy balance can take a giant step backward.

A regular check-in time with your recovering spouse can help keep your fears from taking over. Reflecting often about how things are going, what kind of interactions you're having and how your spouse reports feeling can help you both observe any trends. Intentionally monitoring your own feelings, thoughts and experiences as well can help you keep perspective. You can be more accurate in discerning how things are going and put your fears to rest when you realize that your spouse's bad mood is simply a bad mood and not a return to depression.

A healthy relationship requires both partners to be honest about their feelings and concerns. You and your spouse will make greater progress in returning your marriage to a healthy state when you're able to say, gently and without blame, "I feel scared when I see you sleeping late, withdrawing or having trouble with decisions. I'm afraid the depression might come back again." When these feelings are out in the open, it's easier to evaluate whether these fears have any basis in reality, and it will be easier for your spouse to understand where you're coming from.

FOR REFLECTION

What is my level of comfort with my spouse's recovery? Do I have fears the depression will return? Do these fears harm the recovery process?

How can I best keep track of my spouse's improvement? Am I comfortable with journaling? Would it be easier to write in long hand, keep a computer file or use a voice recorder?

How well are my spouse and I communicating about progress? How can we improve our communication?

TIME TO HEAL

During recovery time, it's important that you continue paying attention to your own needs. You are in recovery every bit as much as your spouses is, and you need to allow yourself time to heal—physically, emotionally and spiritually. Look for ways to relax and recuperate, whether it be through a weekend retreat or simply a daily walk in a park. Continue to ask for and accept help from family and friends.

It's also important to maintain relationships with close friends and family during the recovery process. The people who supported you through your spouse's illness can be a great support system as you both work your way back to health and wholeness. They were in on the worst times and will appreciate being allowed to share in the new good times as well. If you've established a relationship with a prayer partner, a pastor, a Stephen Minister or a Bible study group, make sure that relationship continues.

If you're doing all these things and still find that you and your spouse are struggling to find a healthy, happy relationship, seeking the help of a professional therapist can be very valuable. Though it may be hard to find the time, money and energy to devote to marriage counseling, it's worth the investment. You've made a commitment to this relationship, and you both deserve to get the most out of it, no matter how much trouble it might be to work your way back to a strong marriage.

One other area of your life may also be in need of some recovery: your relationship with God. While the relief of recovery may come as a sign of God's caring involvement, the swamp of depression may have caused you to doubt God's love. And you may be feeling guilty over times when your relationship with God suffered due to your sense of abandonment. Consider Jesus' parable of the Lost Son (see Luke 15:1-31). This father loved his son unconditionally, so that no absence or behavior on the son's part could change that love. God's love for you is just as unlimited. Nothing you do can separate you from God's love. When you return, no matter how long the estrangement or for what reason, God will rejoice and welcome you home.

However, after living through difficult, painful times, not everyone experiences a return to faith and relationship with God. If concerns about your faith still trouble you in the time of recovery, it may help to seek counseling from a minister or a spiritual director. Support from others who have themselves struggled with faith can be a great comfort.

Good times can return to your life again. When the right combination of time, support, medication and therapy all work together to effect your spouse's recovery, more than one life is healed. Yes, you will still need to remain vigilant. You will need to be intentional about monitoring ups and downs. But as light returns to your family's life again, you can also rejoice with the words of David: "Weeping may linger for the night, but joy comes with the morning" (Psalm 30:5).

FOR REFLECTION

How do I feel about the future right now?

What challenges do I see in our relationship during this period of recovery? Are they so difficult that we should consider marriage counseling?

How am I feeling about my relationship with God? Do I need to do something to repair or improve it?

CONCLUSION
LIFE AFTER DEPRESSION

—

It is possible for a couple to come through depression and live a renewed and happy life. When that new time comes, it can be full of joy, surprises and a deeper understanding of what is truly important. God made all creation good, and God can use even depression to bring about good. Depression—when met with prayer, affirmation, community and truth—can also reveal resilience, intimacy, friendship and peace.

BERNADETTE'S STORY

When Ed began to get better, it became evident that we were on a road of discovery and joy. He would wake each morning feeling good inside. He was alive. The depression was gone, and the whole world awaited him. The singing in the shower returned. His hobby of model railroading reawakened. His interest in everything blossomed. Suddenly there were not enough hours in the day to express love to his children and wife, to have fun with his friends, to interact with his fellow workers. He was in love with life, a life given back to him after so many years of depression.

I was the happy recipient of that joy. Not only did I have someone back to help parent the children, I had my lover and best friend again. This, of course, is not to say that we don't have our moments. Ed and I still have disagreements. We still have our moods. But at least we know they will pass, that these are things every married couple experiences from time to time. And we are most appreciative of what we gained during that time of depression.

We came to realize that we could deal with this illness together and with the support of God and our community. I saw Ed in a whole different light. Here was a good man who had hurt deeply yet allowed himself to be vulnerable in order to heal. For me, depression awakened strengths I didn't know I had. I came to know a God who was indeed willing to walk with me every step of the way and yet a God who was not afraid to open my eyes to ways in which I needed to grow. As Ed got better, I recognized the areas of my own growth I had allowed to become fallow during his depression. Ed's recovery challenged me to change.

AMY'S STORY

Even when we knew Bruce had finally found the right combination of therapist and new-generation antidepressant, it took a long time for him to gain enough confidence to enter fully into life again. Over the period of a year, we slowly started noticing changes for the better: He was thinking more clearly and taking on more responsibility; we were all laughing more and enjoying being together; he was beginning to think about the future again. The bickering, hurt feelings and frustration that had marked our lives while he lived under the cloud of depression began to fade away.

Before long, Bruce was working with special-needs students in our local school district. As he re-discovered the gifts he had to offer these hurting children, his emotional health continued to improve. Where he had been morose and negative, he was now bright and animated. He enjoyed the camaraderie of his co-workers, the challenges of his work and having a purpose every day. He and I shared these joys and also helped each other through the concerns we each brought home from work. As things kept getting better, we discovered anew how to lean on each other in parenting, in friendship, in the ups and downs of life.

There were bumps along the way, of course, even after I began to trust the fact of his recovery. After all those years of illness and heartache, it wasn't easy for me to take things at face value. Bruce had to learn to trust himself as well. We still have to remind ourselves often that depression always lurks and that we must be vigilant for signs of its return. But this possibility doesn't dampen our new happiness. We've learned that God does indeed watch over and care for us and has done so all along, even when we were too hurt and frightened to realize it.

—

Though it may be hard to believe or understand, depression in a spouse can actually be a path to happiness. When depression first strikes, it is overwhelming in its darkness and bleakness. We can think only of all we might lose, including our spouse, our best friend, our family, even our own mental health. We feel burdened by the prospect of becoming the sole breadwinner, the single parent, a lonely soul in a broken relationship. Worst of all, we see no end in sight as we watch our spouse fall deeper and deeper into the darkness.

We pray to a God who may seem distant and unhearing. But as avenues of recovery appear, we realize that God was there for us all along. We hear God whisper, through the voice of our suffering spouse or through the friends and family around us, that life is indeed good, that we are God's beloved child and that somehow we will see the light once again. At some point we recognize God's presence as we face each moment of truth: the loneliness of depression, our fears for the future, the actions we take that help or hinder our relationship with our husband or wife.

And then one beautiful moment, light breaks through. Perhaps it comes in a long-missing smile from our spouse, or when we observe a spontaneous moment of play between our spouse and our children. Perhaps it comes in a moment at church when God's presence is felt in a spouse's hug during the greeting of peace. Perhaps it is in a quiet time in bed with a whispered "I love you." Whatever form it takes, the light of healing and renewal appears and then grows brighter.

Even when the end result of our spouse's depression is a permanently broken relationship—from divorce or suicide—God still gives us the opportunity for growth and healing. We can move on to a renewed and happy life when we are able to recognize the strength we brought to the relationship, acknowledge the toll the illness took on our spouse and ourselves, celebrate the gifts we received through our relationship, and let go of any guilt feelings we might have concerning the loss of our loved one.

Henri Nouwen, a Catholic priest and spiritual writer, said, "Every time there are losses, there are choices to be made. You choose to live your losses as passages to anger, blame, hatred, depression and resentment, or you choose to let these losses be a passage to something new, something wider and deeper." With or without our spouse, we have the choice to welcome the light of healing and growth or to continue to live in darkness. Choosing the light opens the door to new and growing experiences. We come to know ourselves better. We come to know our families better. We come to know our God better. We turn outward to accept the help and support of others, growing through openness and honesty. We turn upward and realize that our relationship with our God is deepening, and we pray with St. Francis, "Where there is darkness, let me sow light."

ACKNOWLEDGMENTS

The writers would like to thank all the men and women who shared their stories for this book. Their courage opened the door to understanding the challenges of living with a depressed spouse. Thanks, also, to Dr. Ken Sonnenschein and Dr. Stephen Samuelson for their time and insights. Lastly, a note of appreciation for the staff at ACTA Publications, who included us as partners in the publishing process.